David M. Barnes, Andrew Dickson White

The Draft Riots in New York, July, 1863

The Metropolitan Police, their Services During Riot Week and their

Honorable Record

David M. Barnes, Andrew Dickson White

The Draft Riots in New York, July, 1863
The Metropolitan Police, their Services During Riot Week and their Honorable Record

ISBN/EAN: 9783337306571

Printed in Europe, USA, Canada, Australia, Japan

Cover: Foto ©Suzi / pixelio.de

More available books at **www.hansebooks.com**

THE DRAFT RIOTS IN NEW YORK.

JULY, 1863.

THE

METROPOLITAN POLICE:

THEIR SERVICES DURING RIOT WEEK.

THEIR HONORABLE RECORD.

BY

DAVID M. BARNES.

NEW YORK:

BAKER & GODWIN, PRINTERS AND PUBLISHERS,

PRINTING-HOUSE SQUARE, OPPOSITE CITY HALL.

1863.

To the Board of Police Commissioners—Messrs. Acton and Bergen—Superintendent, Inspectors, and the Officers and Members of the Metropolitan Police of the City of New York, this compilation is respectfully inscribed. It affords Historical Record of the excellence of the organization, of its fidelity, bravery, and efficiency.

DAVID M. BARNES.

New York, Sept., 1863.

PREFATORY.

THE following compilation is a record of facts relating to the operations of the Police during the memorable "Riot Week," embracing an account of the riots, and scenes and incidents connected therewith. The articles were prepared for the *New York Times,* and are reprinted nearly as therein appearing.

The riots commenced on Monday morning, July 13, and were not entirely suppressed until the following Friday. The only protection the city had, on the outbreak, was the Metropolitan Police,—all the regularly organized militia regiments being off in the service of the Government.

The riot which commenced on the first day of the Draft was ostensibly in opposition to it, but early took the character of an outbreak for the purposes of pillage, and also of outrage upon the colored population. For the first three days business in the city was almost entirely suspended, the railroads and omnibuses ceased running, the stores on Broadway, the avenues, and throughout the greater portion of the city were closed, and prowling gangs of ruffians rendered it unsafe to walk the streets.

The services of the Metropolitan Police, officers and men, during Riot Week, won for them the admiration and confidence of the community. Never did men meet an emergency so fearful with more promptness, unanimity, and courage, and never was hazardous and prolonged duty discharged with more willingness and fidelity. There was no flinching or faltering in any quarter, and to their courageous and unaided efforts on Monday and Tuesday can be attributed the safety of the more valuable portions of the city. The riot broke upon them unexpectedly, and when they were the only force to meet it; rallying on sudden warning, they did meet it, and, by their well-concerted action, their speedy movements, and their determined assaults upon the mobs in the different localities, they gave the rioters no time to correctly estimate their own strength or properly estimate the weakness, at the time, of the authorities. Had it not been for this, there is scarce a doubt that the greater excesses which were in contemplation, the raid into the lower portions of the city, the pillaging visit to Wall Street and the Government buildings, would have been consummated, and a period of destruction, plunder, and carnage have ensued to an extent most fearful, and to which what did occur would have been as nothing.

On Tuesday afternoon the police were strengthened by the military, and then commenced exemplary work with the rioters; on all but two or three occasions the military fired directly into the mobs, and with deadly effect. The number killed by the police and the military in the different conflicts, when alone and united, can never be ascertained; it is estimated by those who witnessed the terrible scenes, and have the best opportunity of judging, at from four hundred to five hundred. The bodies of those killed on the spot were hurriedly taken off, and, in many cases, conveyed out of the city, or secreted here and privately buried. Cases of subsequent deaths from wounds, it is known, were attributed to other causes. Eighteen persons are known to have been killed by the rioters, eleven of whom were colored.

The number of buildings burned by the mob, from Monday morning until Wednesday morning, was over fifty,—among them the Colored Orphan Asylum, two Police Stations, three Provost Marshal's Offices, and an entire block of dwellings on Broadway.

A large number of stores and dwellings were sacked, though not burned, and their contents destroyed or carried away. The aggregate amount of property destroyed and stolen amounts to upwards of one million two hundred thousand dollars.

THE METROPOLITAN POLICE.

Their Services during the Riot Week,

JULY, 1863.

THEIR HONORABLE RECORD.

THE acts of the Inspectors, a record of which follows, and their commands, were all conducted under the direction of the Police Commissioners. The legal organization of the Board invests the Superintendent with the command of the force, the Commissioners acting in an administrative capacity. In the absence of the Superintendent the command is assigned to the President of the Board, and thus the duties of Mr. KENNEDY, who early on Monday morning was disabled by the rioters, were assumed by

COMMISSIONER THOMAS C. ACTON

with the promptness, intelligence, and energy which characterize him. The labor during the first four days was immense, and some estimate of it may be formed by the fact that, in the telegraphic department alone, there were upward of *four thousand* dispatches received and orders sent, all of which, with but few exceptions, required the personal supervision of Mr. ACTON. These, it must be remembered, were only a fraction of the many matters requiring his attention. He was not out of the office, save on official business, and then but briefly, during the first five days of the week—the duration of riot and its symptoms—and had no sleep from six o'clock Monday morning until two o'clock on Friday morning. He then lay down for the first time, getting two hours' rest. The position of affairs was one as important and as critical as that on a field of battle; time of as much value; sagacity and decision as necessary. Upward of two thousand men under his control, constant emergencies being attacked.   Inspector CARPENTER at once took command of a force of two hundred.   Before leaving he addressed his men, telling them they "*had* to meet and *to put down* a mob; to take no prisoners; to strike quick and strike hard."   A speedy march was taken to and up Broadway, and when the force reached Bond Street a body of rioters was seen marching down and near to Amity.   They bore a huge board banner, inscribed "No Draft," and desecrated the American flag by bearing it in their midst.   The two forces sighted each other unexpectedly.   The rioters, fresh from the attempted sacking of Mayor OPDYKE's house, had marched from Fourteenth Street down Broadway, armed with clubs, pitchforks, iron bars, swords, and many with guns and pistols.   Every colored man they met had been abused and mercilessly beaten.   Terror seized pedestrians and storekeepers; the former hurried out of the way; the latter hastily closed and barred doors and windows.   Vehicles turned to the right and left, and to a thousand vile-visaged and lawless men the undisputed right of way was surrendered.   The intention of this gang, openly avowed, was to enter the Lafarge House, where colored servants were employed, and do havoc to them and it.   Most fortunately, police protection was at hand.   Quick as thought, on the first glimpse of them, Inspector CARPENTER gave the successive orders, just in front of the Lafarge, "By the right flank! Company, front! Double quick, charge!" and, with upraised clubs, in splendid order did they obey.   Inspector CARPENTER, with reckless but characteristic courage, was far ahead of his command, and, for a moment, among the mob single and alone.   He had the first blow, drew the first blood, selecting for his victim a powerfully built ruffian, defiantly brandishing his club; a terrific blow upon his head from the Inspector, and he was left to the attention of others, while Mr. CARPENTER, with the men now beside him, went in for a literal fulfillment of his order on leaving headquarters.   The mob, bewildered at the sudden meeting, staggered at the outset by the determined onset of the police, were unable to rally for effective fight.   The clubs flew rapidly and surely upon devoted heads, a score lay prostrate upon the street, two were killed, the "No Draft" banner captured and destroyed, and the "Stars and Stripes" made prize of and carried in the ranks of those who, by word or deed, would never dishonor them.   In five minutes the victory was complete, and the ruffians, save those who lay in the streets, dispersed in all directions, leaving strewn around weapons, villainous and of all descriptions.   The contest was witnessed by thousands, cheers greeted the police on their charge, and after the fight they were renewed with double earnestness.   This was the first regular fight with the mob. The force did not know how many they were meeting, nor did they care; and nobly was their courage vindicated.   Inspector CARPENTER incurred arising in all sections of the city, immediate action required on information received, and five minutes' delay leading to disaster, Commissioner ACTON was equal to his situation, exhibiting wonderful powers of endurance, and a coolness, activity, and vigor which on every occasion led to success; these were the more noticeable from the fact that, as Superintendent *ex-officio*, his post was a new and untried one, full of the gravest responsibilities. He assumed it suddenly, met all the trying emergencies promptly and sagaciously, won the confidence of the community, and covered himself with honor by the results.

Fortunately, between the military acting with them and the police entire unanimity prevailed, and orders wherein the two were required were obeyed with alacrity and with concert of feeling and purpose. It is worthy of note that every expedition—large and small there were over fifty—sent out by Commissioner ACTON, whether of the police singly, or the military and police conjoined, was successful, beating and dispersing the mobs, and saving lives and property; in short, fully accomplishing the purposes for which they were dispatched. To Commissioner ACTON are our citizens indebted in a large degree for the prompt and successful assaults upon the rioters, and to his judicious and energetic action for their subsequent entire defeat and dispersion.

In the discharge of the manifold duties at headquarters,

COMMISSIONER JOHN G. BERGEN

was prominent. His duties were no less responsible than those of Mr. ACTON, and not unfrequently he relieved the latter in the disposition of the forces. He was almost constantly at headquarters during the period of tremor and excitement, and exhibited, to a marked degree, his peculiarities of coolness, prompt conclusions, and steady perseverance. He came through the trying labors, the wearying days and nights, fresh as at the outset, exhibiting a wonderful capacity to sustain fatigue. The principal responsibility resting upon Mr. BERGEN was that of the care of Brooklyn, and to this his anxieties and energies were chiefly directed. How well he succeeded in its preservation from lawlessness is evidenced in the fact that, though there were many indications of serious disturbances there, yet the police in that section, acting under his orders, were successful in all, but one single instance, in suppressing them.

Mr. BERGEN was indefatigable; cautious and intelligent in all his acts, he added largely to the efficiency and strength of the Department, and contributed greatly to the successes which have won for it so much of honor.

The force of Clerks at headquarters is about thirteen, and all of these were steadily employed during the riots, exhibiting a faithfulness to duty and willingness to assume it, however prolonged and heavy, which was most creditable. They were under the supervision of

CHIEF CLERK SETH C. HAWLEY,

whose duties were multifarious, constant, and wearying, and who, for a week from Monday, when the riot commenced, allowed himself no rest but that of one hour in the twenty-four. Having the supervision of the clerks and special patrolmen, the providing and issuing of arms, the execution of orders from the Commissioners, seeing to the wounded and providing for the refugees, disposing of the prisoners, and acting as commissary for over four thousand of police, military, and specials assembled at headquarters—these were only a portion of the multitudinous duties he was called upon to assume. He performed an amount of work, satisfactorily and thoroughly, which would have staggered any man of less capacity and energy. He proved himself eminently adapted for his position, and was of invaluable service to the Commissioners and the public.

THE NEW HEADQUARTERS

deserve, in this connection, mention. Their advantage and capacity were thoroughly tested. From first to last, there were upward of two thousand policemen there, all the military, acting in conjunction with them, two thousand special patrolmen, colored refugees from the mob to the number of seven hundred, and hundreds of prisoners. All these had to be housed and fed in the building, and all were so housed and fed without confusion or discomfort. Had these headquarters not existed, and the old ones been in use, it would have been impossible to have afforded accommodations of any kind, and it is more than likely that all attempts to concentrate others than the police, or, if concentrated, to retain them, would have wholly failed. The wisdom of erecting the headquarters, which some have deemed an extravagance, has been fully demonstrated.

SUPERINTENDENT JOHN A. KENNEDY.

Although there had been, for a few days preceding the Riot Week, inklings of disturbance, there was nothing, save the report on Saturday afternoon that the Seventh Avenue Arsenal was to be attacked, which rendered necessary any other than the ordinary precaution of vigilance. The rumor in reference to the arsenal, slight as it was, induced the

Superintendent to send fifty men to guard it, with orders to remain until relieved. Subsequent events proved his wisdom, for this action prevented the earlier commencement of the riots and their more formidable character. It has been ascertained that there was a well concerted plan to sack the arsenal on Saturday or Sunday night, and to procure the arms and ammunition. Thus provided, the mob would have displayed a far more formidable front on Monday, and more steadily, boldly, and bloodily defied the attempts to subdue it.

Until Monday after 7 A. M. Mr. KENNEDY heard nothing, beyond the rumor on which he had so promptly acted, which excited any apprehension. About that hour, however, he snuffed riot in the fact communicated to him that the Street Contractor's men in the Nineteenth Ward were not at work. His first thought, as it was draft day in some districts, was for the safety of Provost Marshal MANIERRE'S office, No. 1190 Broadway, and Marshal JENKINS' office, Forty-sixth Street and Third Avenue, and he accordingly telegraphed to several of the upper precincts for detachments of men to report forthwith to Captain PORTER, of the Nineteenth, for protection of JENKINS' office, and dispatched another force to report to Captain SPEIGHT, of the Twenty-ninth, for duty at MANIERRE'S office. Meantime further rumors of riotous disposition had reached him, and he promptly issued orders to the different precincts to immediately assemble their reserve force. When it is remembered that this is half the entire force, and the men, going off duty at 6 A. M., are scattered here, there, and everywhere, the labor devolved on the officers of the different precincts can well be imagined. The force gathered in strength, however, at headquarters, during the afternoon.

Superintendent KENNEDY, having dispatched more men to Captain SPEIGHT, and perfected, so far as was then deemed necessary, every arrangement, started about 10 A. M. on a tour for personal inspection of the districts reported infected. Visiting Captain SPEIGHT and the Seventh Avenue Arsenal, and leaving directions for any emergency, he drove across town; noticing a fire at Third Avenue and Forty-sixth Street, left his wagon and walked toward it. The Superintendent was not in uniform, had no insignia of any kind, and was wholly unarmed. As he passed along Forty-sixth Street he observed that every face was radiant with gratification; every person seemed to be highly pleased; no evidences were exhibited of a disposition to riot, or to any mischievous conduct, when some one exclaimed : "There's KENNEDY !" and to a query : "Which is him ?" he was pointed out. He took no notice of this, but, on being pushed violently against by a returned soldier, wheeled round and demanded what that was for ; received a violent blow in the face from one of the crowd suddenly gathering on him, which knocked him over and down an embankment some six feet high. This was the signal for the cowardly fury of the mob, and down they rushed for him; instantly regaining his feet, he put himself to his speed across lots toward Forty-seventh Street, and had gained on his yelling, maniacal pursuers; had reached and ascended the embankment; but foes, equally as cowardly and brutal, met him here; the attack and pursuit had been seen from the opposite embankment, and with cool malignity a crowd awaited his coming; he had but just gained the top of it, when a rush was made upon him, and a powerful blow sent him headlong back again, prostrate at the very feet of his original assailants. He felt throughout that his safety was in keeping his feet, and instantly was he again upon them, but too late for another run for life; the mob, with its Forty-seventh Street reinforcement, closed on him with yells of exultation, dealing upon him blows with fists and feet. One fellow, armed with a heavy club, made earnest and numerous efforts to dash his brains out; but the Superintendent, having a careful eye to them and a quick one for the ruffian's movements, managed to keep his head "well in hand," dodge his blows, and all others aimed at that quarter, with wonderful dexterity. During this terrific ordeal some fifty blows on all parts of his body must have been received. In the swaying about of the mob and its victim, they had moved toward Lexington Avenue, and close to a wide mud-hole; into this a tremendous blow behind the ear sent the Superintendent head foremost, with great violence; here it was where his face, buried amid the mud and stones, received the terrible injuries which rendered him unrecognizable. Then arose a jubilant cheer, and the mob yelled, "Drown him! drown him!" But the Superintendent proved that a plucky, determined man has nine lives as well as a cat. Marvelously enough, even now, he retained his consciousness, was once more promptly on his feet, and exhibited a neat bit of strategy and agility. The mud was too deep, the pond too wide, for the villains to enter in or pursue through; they were on the Forty-sixth Street side; the Superintendent took in the situation at a glance, and made straight across the pond for Lexington Avenue again; this gave him, on reaching the other side, an advantageous start of his pursuers, who had to chase around the borders, and who, on seeing themselves thus outgeneraled, came after him with redoubled yells and execrations. They were too late, however. He reached, in advance, the Lexington Avenue embankment, sprung up it, and recognizing near by Mr. JOHN EAGAN, a well-known and influential resident of the vicinity, exclaimed to him, "JOHN EAGAN, come here and save my life!" He was now covered with blood and mud, and unrecognizable. EAGAN came promptly to his relief, and had influence enough to keep the mob back, who—Mr. KENNEDY'S strength now succumbing, and he presenting an appearance of having little if any life left—were the more readily restrained because of their belief that " he was as good as a dead man." Mr. Eagan and one or two others secured a feed wagon, placed Mr. Kennedy in it, and at once conveyed him to headquarters. Mr. Eagan did not know for whom his powerful and disinterested effort had been made until after driving some distance from the scene.

The unexpected arrival of Mr. Kennedy in such a condition created the most intense excitement and indignation. He was almost unconscious, his face fearfully bruised and cut, one eye entirely closed, lips swelled frightfully—in short, not John A. Kennedy's visage in any particular—his hand cut with a knife, his body a mass of bruises, and his person covered with blood and mud. From headquarters, after surgical care, he was taken to the house of a friend, and so soon as a thorough examination showed that no bones were broken or internal injury sustained, he was, despite remonstrance, on his feet again, and on Thursday of the same week attending to duties at the office. He bears yet the scars of his encounter ; but as they are marks of honor, however inconvenient, he can patiently wear them till time wipes them off.

Mr. Kennedy is sixty years of age,—a fact suggestive of the vile and cowardly character of his assailants, as well as of the iron constitution which has brought him through. Of his great self-possession and determination, the facts detailed afford the evidence.

Owing to the early injuries, as detailed, of Superintendent Kennedy, on Monday, the Department was deprived of his intelligent and energetic action, and the duties, under supervision of Commissioner Acton, to a great degree devolved upon

INSPECTOR DANIEL CARPENTER.

He was busily engaged in perfecting the orders issued by Mr. Kennedy when the latter was brought into headquarters bruised, bleeding, and unconscious. This was the first confirmation received there of formidable disturbance. With approval of Commissioner Acton, Mr. Carpenter at once telegraphed for the immediate massing of the entire force at headquarters. The orders were obeyed with alacrity, and by 3 o'clock P. M. a large number were assembled. The wisdom of this measure subsequent events fully proved.

Further confirmation of the riot and its proportions meantime had reached headquarters, and the men were being rapidly organized, formed into companies, and put under different commanders. About 4 P. M. word was received that Mayor Opdyke's house, in Fifth Avenue, was a risk for which he might have paid the penalty of his life, and it is wonderful he did not; but he escaped uninjured, and left record on heads and bodies which will be long borne and remembered.

Immediately reforming his men, and cool as though naught had happened, he marched to the Mayor's house, Fifth Avenue; but finding all quiet, returned to headquarters. Reports of the fight on Broadway had reached there, and, on the appearance of himself and force with the captured flag, they were greeted with enthusiastic cheers.

The Inspector's rest here was but brief, for, at 8 P. M., it was reported that the *Tribune* Buildings were to be attacked. At once taking command of two hundred men—one hundred from Brooklyn, under Inspector FOLK—he marched rapidly for and down Broadway, entering the Park just as the mob, which had been repulsed from the *Tribune* Build ings by the police of the lower precincts, were fleeing across it; instantly divining the situation, he formed "company front," and swept the Park, to Printing-house Square, on the double-quick—the fleeing rioters, who were rushing from one punishment to another, receiving the clubs terribly, and being knocked in all directions. The square at and around the *Times* office being entirely clear, Inspector CARPENTER took up his quarters at the City Hall; soon after he was weakened by the withdrawal of Inspector FOLK and one hundred men, who were ordered to Brooklyn. A report reaching him that the negro shanties in Baxter Street were being fired, he detailed Capt. JOURDAN, of the Sixth Precinct, with a force, to visit that section, which he right bravely did, dispersing crowds and preventing contemplated destruction. Subsequently word came that negro dwellings were being sacked and burned in the Fourth Ward, in Dover Street and its vicinity. Fifty men were left to act in case of a renewed attack upon the *Tribune* Buildings, and with the balance Inspector CARPENTER marched to the new scene of violence. He came, unawares, upon a large mob engaged in pillaging and firing dwellings, caught them on the double-quick, and administered terrible punishment. At four different places in this Ward were mobs at their work—burning, pillaging, and beating. Inspector CARPENTER, with his force, marched from one to the other, making sudden onslaughts, dispersing the rioters, and extinguishing fires. In many cases the villains were chased into houses, and had to escape from the windows or receive unsparingly the locust.

An incident occurred during these engagements which excited the ire and nerved still more the arm of the police. Three colored men had fled to the roof of a dwelling to escape the rioters, who subsequently fired it in the upper story. The flames, reaching the roof, drove the poor fellows from it, and when the police arrived they were seen sus-

pended against the side of the building, clinging to the gable-end.
Every effort was made by Inspector CARPENTER and his men to rescue
them, but no ladders or means to do so could be procured, and becom-
ing exhausted, they successively fell to the ground—one of them, whom
the fire had reached, with his clothes in flames. Each one was badly injured, but all were placed in care and safety.

After the effective work in the Fourth Ward, Inspector CARPENTER
returned with his gallant command to the City Hall; he had scarcely
reached there—it was now 11 P. M.—ere word was received of a mob
coming down Broadway for another attack upon the *Tribune* Buildings;
Mr. CARPENTER at once massed what of his force were left close to the
east gate of the Park, facing three companies to the west, from which
direction he knew the mob would come, and the balance to the east.
They did come with yells, shouts, and dire intent. The force was concealed by the darkness, and, unsuspectingly, the rioters marched into the
trap laid for them. They were some four hundred strong, and were allowed to get within one hundred yards ere Inspector CARPENTER gave
the orders, "Up, Guards, and at them!" Well and overwhelmingly was
he obeyed, and against far greater numbers; every man was knocked
down who could be reached. The Park was strewn with the prostrate,
the ranks broken, the mob fleeing, and the police were again masters of
the situation.

This ended, for Inspector CARPENTER and his command, their duties
for the night—constant and arduous, and most gallantly performed. He
was relieved at midnight by Inspector LEONARD and force, and returned
with his men to headquarters.

On Tuesday morning, at 6 o'clock, with two hundred and fifty men,
Inspector CARPENTER proceeded to Second Avenue; on reaching it at
Twenty-first Street the force were met with groans and hooting, but by
no assault, until passing the block between Thirty-second and Thirty-
third Streets; here the rear of the force was suddenly assailed with
showers of bricks, stones, and other missiles, from the roofs and windows of the adjoining houses; several of the men were knocked down;
two were badly injured; the Inspector instantly halted his command,
and directed a force of fifty to storm the houses, enter to the roofs, and
render *hors du combat* every one engaged in the assault. The order was
obeyed with a cheer, the locked and barricaded doors broken in and
forced, the premises entered, all resistants knocked down, the roofs
reached, where were found a large number of the assailants. Here a
hand-to-hand and desperate fight ensued, in which the ruffians were overcome and several fearfully punished; many were left lying on the roofs,
others fled through the scuttles only to receive the clubs of the officers

in wait below, and those who escaped into the street were met by the reserve, who administered severe retribution. The victory was complete, the houses thoroughly cleared, and the missiles cast from the roofs into the street. Reforming his force, march was made through the infected streets and avenues without meeting further opposition, and thence to headquarters at 1 P. M. The afternoon was here spent by the Inspector in attending to duties created by the emergency.

At 9 P. M., receiving word of an attack being made on BROOKS BROTHERS' clothing store, Catharine Street, with one hundred and fifty men he hastened to the scene, arriving too late to prevent the sacking, but taking an active part in the punishment and dispersion of the mob in and around the building. Thence leading his command through the several infested streets of that vicinity, they were cleared of all disturbers. While thus engaged, word came that a renewed attack upon the *Tribune* was anticipated, and forthwith he hastened to the Park ; here, finding the report was unfounded, but hearing that a mob had threatened the sugar-house on Leonard Street, and was then sacking negro houses in its vicinity, he immediately moved his command to that quarter, and coming suddenly upon, charged the crowd while at their work of pillage, and routed them with many a broken skull ; thence a hurried march was made to York Street, where riotous demonstrations had been made, but the mob broke and dispersed as they appeared. Thus closed another night of unceasing and arduous duty performed by Inspector CARPENTER and his well-worked men, and well-working men.

Wednesday brought relief to the Inspector from out-door duty, but he was unceasingly engaged, day and night, at headquarters, in the multifarious matters requiring attention. His thorough knowledge of the Department and its resources, his correct judgment and great decision of character, were of incalculable service to the Department and the public.

On Thursday morning Inspector CARPENTER was directed by Commissioner ACTON to accompany Capt. PUTNAM, of the regulars, with his command, through avenues and streets infected, and report condition. The centers of the riotous districts were visited. No indications of further disturbance existed, but every store was closed, people anxiously peering, as the military passed, from doors and windows. The Inspector announced to all that the "reign of terror" was over and that they could resume their business with the assurance of being protected ; similar assurances were given to the railroad and omnibus companies in that section which had not resumed running. A halt was made at the Twenty-first Precinct Station-house, when Mr. CARPENTER heard that two of the force, wounded, were secreted in a house in East Forty-third

Street, fearful of coming out.   Capt. PUTNAM accompanied the Inspector to the premises where it was ascertained that the wounded men had been secreted, but, being furnished with citizens' clothes, had subsequently escaped.

A slow return was made from Forty-third Street, over the section so recently one of riot.   Scouts were sent out by the Inspector on either side of the line of march, who brought back word of "all quiet," and at 1 P. M. headquarters were reached, Mr. CARPENTER returning "all quiet" as the gratifying report.

From that time until Saturday noon he was on duty at the office, not having, from Monday morning, but three hours at his own house.

Thus closes the record of Inspector CARPENTER during "Riot Week." On all occasions, and in all positions where intelligence, sagacity, and manly courage were required, Inspector CARPENTER evinced them.   His duties and responsibilities were largely increased by the early injuries to Superintendent KENNEDY, but he proved equal to all of them, and has added to his repute as an invaluable officer.   On all occasions he was nobly seconded by the men under his command, and he refers with pride to their fidelity and effectiveness.

After confirmation of the riot reached headquarters, the utmost activity prevailed there, and, under supervision of Commissioner ACTON, every effort was made to rapidly gather the men.   To organize them when gathered, put them under proper commands, prepare them for any emergency, and speed them to the different points where needed, was a work of unceasing labor.   During the day and night of Monday,

INSPECTOR GEORGE W. DILKS

was incessantly occupied in aiding to do this, and brought to the work the advantage of a long and active experience in the Department, a quick appreciation of the necessities of the occasion, and an energy and zeal which never flagged.   He was thus unceasingly engaged until 10 o'clock A. M. of Tuesday, when he was ordered to the command of two hundred men, and to march forthwith to the protection of the Wire Factory at Twenty-second Street and Second Avenue [where some four thousand carbines were stored], which was reported as being attacked. A rapid march was made to Twenty-first Street, thence into the avenue. On wheeling into and up it, they encountered a mob, swelled to thousands.   They had forced the factory, the arms were being taken out, and scores were already provided with them.   Exultant over such plunder, the rioters greeted the appearance of the force with shouts of derision and defiance.   For Inspector DILKS to throw his command upon such

2

overwhelming numbers was full of hazard; to retreat before them, full of danger. Not a moment was to be lost, and, instantly forming his men, he ordered a rapid charge. The mob, for a while, stood its ground, and hand-to-hand encounters ensued, of which the Inspector had his full share; orders had been given to recapture all the stolen guns, and squads of the force charged for them at different points into the mob, mowing their way in and back against weighty odds. The proportions and fierce character of this fight on the one hand, and the courage on the other, made it the severest encounter of the week. The ground was strewn with men, on sidewalks, in the gutters, and on the street, bleeding and senseless. At last brute courage yielded to determined bravery and steady discipline. The mob, broken and terrified, fled, leaving Inspector Dilks and his command masters of the ground. Thus ended the engagement " on the field," in which many of the force were injured, but not one faltered.

To the factory now, which was filled with rioters, still pillaging it of arms and determined to defend it, instant attention was turned. Wheeling his men to the front, Inspector Dilks gave the orders to assault and *take* it. The entrance was forced, the stairs won step by step, and the building cleared, but only after savage and continuous fighting, in which serious punishment was inflicted by the police; men laid throughout the factory, victims of their own lawlessness, and the bloody marks of the contest were on all parts of the building. Those who escaped from within ran the gauntlet of the force remaining in the street, and few, if any, got away unscathed. The punishment inflicted during these contests was terrible; a physician dressed the wounds of twenty-one of the rioters, all on the head, and all of which he considered fatal.

Having cleared the factory, taken what guns were found there, which, with those recaptured in the street, made one for every man, and the mob not reappearing, Inspector Dilks returned with his force to headquarters. On the way down with their trophies the command were repeatedly cheered, and on reaching "home," at 3 P. M., the force there welcomed them most cordially.

Half an hour after return, word was received that an attack was again being made upon the factory. Inspector Dilks at once took command of another two hundred and, accompanied by Capt. Franklin's company of military, returned to the scene, entering Second Avenue, as before, from Twenty-first Street. Here he discovered Capt. Helm and a small force of police, who had just visited the factory, securing some boxes of arms which had been overlooked. They were being closed in upon from all quarters by a fast-gathering and now intensely infuriated mob, against which they would have been powerless; the timely relief was welcomed with heartiest cheers; the mob, remembering the lessons of but a short time previous, made but a short fight, broke and fled.   Capt. HELM's force joined Inspector DILKS' command; a halt at and final search of the factory, for arms, were made, and march resumed, with the military now taking the right, down Twenty-second Street to First Avenue.   From buildings along the route they were continuously stoned and fired at, making no response save in one instance: a man stood at a window, upraising a huge rock, and just on the point of hurling it into the ranks; he was instantly shot,—the ball entering his head and he falling dead.   On wheeling into First Avenue, a large body of rioters, toward Twenty-first Street, suddenly assailed them, rapidly firing upon them and making the air thick with the hurling stones and other missiles; so obstinate and determinedly continued was this attack that Capt. FRANKLIN, filing his men across and facing down the avenue, warned the rioters to disperse or he should fire upon them; they answered with shouts of defiance and renewed the attack; the word was then given, and several volleys were fired with terrible effect; the crowd fell back, the two forces following, the military firing as they advanced.

At Twenty-first Street, the mob, panic-stricken at the slaughter in their ranks, fled.   A countermarch was made to Twenty-second Street, thence to Second Avenue and to Twenty-first.   Reaching here, the forces were again assailed, receiving a volley from the First Avenue, where the mob, well armed, had speedily reassembled.   Capt. FRANKLIN instantly wheeled and faced his men to meet this unexpected attack, giving immediate orders to fire.   The mob, a block off, stood several discharges, boldly returning them, but at length and after more slaughter, broke and fled.

During this engagement the Inspector had many narrow escapes, one especially so—a Minnié ball striking close to his head and cutting off a tree branch bending near him.

A huge, powerfully built man was noticed at the head of the mob, leaping into the air, wildly swinging his arms and shaking his fists, evidently one of the ringleaders, crazy for riot and blood.   He was singled out, received a shot in the forehead, and fell dead.   Another, who had boldly ventured away from his comrades and advanced up Twenty-first Street, stood gritting his teeth, shaking his fists at and cursing the soldiers, ceasing this only to shout encouragement to the rioters. He literally exhibited demoniac rage.   He was picked out, shot, and fell dead in the midst of his threats and imprecations.

This was the last contest in which Inspector DILKS and his command were engaged on that day, and their position throughout was a trying one.   On the march through Twenty-second Street they acted as skirmishers, doing bold duty and incurring great risks. On both occasions when the military took the offensive they were brought to a halt, the balls and missiles from the mob whistling over and among them, without the opportunity of assault or defence; steady courage was required to endure this. No serious injuries were sustained by the men, and the mob appearing to be entirely dispersed, headquarters were returned to, the party received with cheers, and Capt. HELM's trophies deposited.

All that night, and until Wednesday evening, Inspector DILKS was incessantly on duty at the headquarters. At dusk, on Wednesday, with another force of two hundred, accompanied by Capt. PUTNAM's regulars, the infected district was visited, and a tour through Second and Third Avenues and the intervening streets, from Seventeenth to Twenty-second, was made. First Avenue, from Eighteenth to Twenty-first, was filled with excited people, and there was almost uninterrupted skirmishing the entire distance. Both from the streets and the houses were the military and police fired at, while missiles fell among them thick and fast; two of the force were shot, though not seriously, and numbers were struck with bricks and stones. They advanced slowly and steadily, clearing the street before them,—Inspector DILKS, whenever occasion required, making a charge, in some cases having sharp fighting, and preventing any formidable gathering; the military fired but a few shots, and before the tour was completed the mob had wholly dispersed. Returning to headquarters, Inspector DILKS was occupied in duties there until after midnight, when, for the first time since Monday morning, he took rest and sleep. Subsequently, and until quiet was restored, he was on constant duty, but not again " in the field."

Throughout all the exciting scenes narrated, the courage, coolness, and decision of the Inspector were prominent; there were no duties in which he did not share, no dangers in which he did not lead. He had true and brave men to sustain him, and how zealously, unflinchingly they did so, the record tells.

Of course it is understood that, in the duties performed and in the dangers incurred by the different Inspectors, the forces under their command share equally with them in whatever of honor is attached. This the Inspectors themselves claim; they know that to the bravery of their officers and men, to their eager and constant devotion to duty, are their successes and honors attributable. Each one of them admits this enthusiastically, and none more so than

INSPECTOR JAMES LEONARD.

Inspector LEONARD was on duty at headquarters on Monday when Superintendent KENNEDY was brought in. After Inspector CARPENTER left with his command, acting under orders from Commissioner Acton he was incessantly occupied in massing at headquarters what of the force had not been assembled, and in organizing them. At 9 o'clock P. M. rumors of a mob coming down Broadway were received. Taking command of a force, Inspector Leonard marched to Broadway, met them at Bond Street—near the scene of Inspector Carpenter's afternoon victory —charged upon them, and, after a brief but severe "little fight," broke, punished and dispersed them. Returning to headquarters, he resumed duties there until midnight, when he was ordered, with a force of 350 men, to repair to the City Hall and relieve Inspector Carpenter. While here his work was constant. Acting on information received, he sent forces to Leonard and York Streets, to protect the negroes there, and punish the prowling gangs threatening them. This duty was thoroughly performed, and was the means of saving lives, limbs, and property also. He detailed a force to protect a provision store in Greenwich Street, near Cortlandt, which he learned had been broken open and was being sacked. The mob was attacked, beaten, and dispersed, and much property saved. More of his force was sent to Brooks Brothers' clothing store to aid in its defence. Portions were detailed to protect the hotels in Fulton and Cortlandt Streets, threatened by mobs, the proprietors of which had applied for aid. Toward morning, he received word that a mob was marching to Fulton Ferry to meet the boats and prevent the landing of marines expected from the Navy Yard, and that they also designed burning Fulton Market, from the occupants of which a gang, attempting to kill a negro on the previous day, received severe punishment. Instantly Inspector Leonard sent off a force to defeat their purposes. They met the mob—a formidable one—charged upon it with determined energy, and drove it in all directions.

It was now daylight, and Inspector Leonard, who had reached the Hall with 350 men, had sent off, in obedience to telegraphs from headquarters, so many detachments to divers sections that, by 9 o'clock A. M. of Tuesday, he found himself without a man, and was left alone in his glory. 'Twas quite evident that at headquarters his resources were thought equal to his energy and fidelity, for, at that hour, another order came for another detachment. Being the only detachment left, he personally reported himself as such at headquarters. Representing to Commissioner Acton the necessity for continuing a strong force in the neighborhood of Printing-house Square, he was ordered to the command of 200 men, and with them hurried back to the City Hall. Upon the square and in the Park were thousands of riotously disposed persons, and the evidences of violence were gathering apace ; every unfortunate negro who appeared was chased and beaten, inflammatory speeches were being made, and threats openly uttered.   All these had increased at noon to such an extent that, taking 100 men, Mr. Leonard swept the Park and square, clearing them of the dangerous material ; considerable. opposition was received, but, with the small force of brave spirits, the work was done quickly and thoroughly.   Several times, during the day, had he to disperse the gatherings in these sections, and, by his discretion and firmness, undoubtedly saved a serious demonstration.   At eight o'clock in the evening, a company of regulars, just arrived, were being followed up Broadway by a hooting, yelling mob, who were besliming and endeavoring to intimidate them.   A plan to assault them and prevent their aiding the authorities was evidently perfecting.   Inspector Leonard, accompanied by Sergeant Polly, of the Eleventh Precinct, had met the mob as it passed the west entrance to the Park, and mingled with it until reaching Broadway and Chambers Street ; here danger of an attack by overwhelming numbers was imminent ; to save the soldiers was the first object, and to do that it was necessary to distract the attention of the mob from them.   The plan adopted was one of boldness and hazard : a prominent ringleader was pointed out by the officer in command to Inspector Leonard, who forthwith seized him ; aided by Sergeant Polly and one patrolman, the fellow, offering violent resistance, was dragged into the Park and toward the City Hall ; meantime the *ruse* had had its intended effect ; the entire gang of demons, turning from the soldiers, rushed to the rescue of their leader ; on they came, three hundred against three, but these three determined men.   " Kill them ! kill them !   We'll give you what we gave Kennedy," were their shouts, as surging on they sought to overthrow and rescue.   Facing the infuriates with his prisoner in vice-like grasp, the firm front, the uplifted club, and the plainly speaking determination of Inspector Leonard to " do or die," bravely seconded as he was by his two associates, awed the mob from too close, too dangerous proximity.   Once, however, a rush was made which threatened to overwhelm and crush them ; well-directed, fearless and telling blows stunned and staggered back the foremost ; the prisoner, held in front, and used as a guard against the missiles and blows aimed at the officers, was bleeding from the punishment received from friends as well as foes. Thus, from the Chambers Street entrance to the one from Broadway, ever facing the crowd and keeping it to their front, Inspector Leonard and his aids succeeded in working their way.   Here, and when it was indeed needed, help was at hand, for the mob, now fully realizing the disproportion of strength, were preparing for one final and overwhelming effort.   Fortunately word had reached the City Hall, and seventy-five of the force came rushing to the rescue.   The moment they joined him, the brawny prisoner, whom there was no intention to retain, and who had so well been used for the purposes of the *ruse* and the defence, was cast aside, worthless, bleeding; and in with the reinforcements the Inspector went for exemplary punishment to the mob. A hand-to-hand fight ensued, heads were broken, men prostrated and laid in heaps, and in less time than it is recorded, those who a few moments before were eager for and intent upon the lives of the three daring officers, were scattered like sheep before the gallant charge of the police, or lay as slaughtered. Inspector LEONARD was boldly in the fray, his stalwart form being conspicuous, his rapid, earnestly meant and muscular blows falling with telling effect.

This was the last of the exciting duties in which Inspector LEONARD was engaged. He remained on duty at the Hall, however, until Friday, when, with his officers and men, he was recalled. During his command there he had rendered invaluable services to that section and the lower portion of the city. Constantly on the *qui vive*, sending out scouts and receiving prompt intimation of all designs there and thereabouts, he promptly met and defeated them. He had immense interests to guard; himself a host, his officers and men true as steel, they saved the districts committed to their care from the consummation of well-concocted plans of violence and pillage. Of active intelligence and proved courage, Inspector LEONARD's name shines brightly on the record of honor.

Although Brooklyn escaped scenes similar to those which disgraced and horrified New York, it was evident that the material was there to create them, and nothing but the firm front of

INSPECTOR JOHN S. FOLK,

cordially seconded by his command, and the military and civil authorities, prevented outbreaks. He received a dispatch at 10½ o'clock Monday, from headquarters New York, directing him to call in his reserve, and to hold them in immediate readiness. They were on drill at Fort Green at the time, and forthwith he ordered them to their respective precincts.

At 5 o'clock P. M. a dispatch was received from Commissioner BERGEN to send his whole force to New York, if, in the Inspector's opinion, it would be safe for them to leave Brooklyn. He did think it was safe, and as soon thereafter as headquarters could be reached reported himself at Mulberry Street with upward of two hundred men. On consultation with Commissioners ACTON and BERGEN, it was thought best for him and his command to return to Brooklyn, to be ready for any emergency that might arise there. Before leaving, and about 8 P. M., word came of the demonstration on the *Tribune* Buildings, and Inspector

FOLK was ordered to join his force to that of Inspector CARPENTER, ac
company him as far as the *Tribune* Buildings and render what aid
was required in dispersing the mob thereabouts. On reaching the Park,
the mob—an account of whose flight from Printing-house Square, and
reception in the Park by Mr. CARPENTER's command, has been given—
was severely dealt with by Inspector FOLK and his command, who, being on the left, had the last handling of the fleeing, and they made
havoc, strewing the ground with them, right and left. Inspector FOLK
escaped a huge club by an adroit dodge, and laid the party wielding it
low, only to incur another flying attack, which he met, evaded, and simi-
larly ended. This duty over, and with cheers from Inspector CARPEN-
TER's force, Mr. FOLK at once took up the march for Brooklyn. Reaching Fulton Ferry, he heard that but a short time before two negroes had
been killed on the docks near by. Halting his command and taking a
squad he made inspection of the vicinity, finding on a schooner two negroes, one with his head terribly cut and his arm broken the other only
suffering from body bruises. Inspector FOLK at once took measures to
send the poor fellow most injured to the hospital. He tried to hire two
hacks, offering the drivers to pay what they wanted, and to send a guard
of police with them. One was unwilling to bloody his carriage, and
drove hastily away; the other "had a call," and as rapidly followed.
An omnibus at the ferry was then hailed, but the driver represented that
it might endanger his life and the life of his passengers. The Inspector,
seeing some justice in this, essayed elsewhere and secured a fish wagon.
The wounded man was placed carefully in it, and sent off, under sufficient guard, to the hospital. This done, the force returned to Brooklyn,
and reaching there was dismissed to the several precincts, with directions to hold themselves in readiness on a moment's notice.

From that time until Wednesday night nothing occurred of a serious character. So well had Inspector FOLK instructed his forces, and so
efficiently had they obeyed, that the slightest lawless gatherings were
met and dispersed by the different precinct police and no opportunity
for any demonstration afforded.

At about 11½ o'clock on Wednesday evening the elevators in the
basin were fired, and to them at once Inspector FOLK and his command
hastened. Meeting an immense crowd of citizens and firemen near the
scene, the latter opened as they came on the double-quick and gave them
cheer on cheer as they hurried through. On reaching the immediate
vicinity of the fire they were greeted with groans and hisses, but with no
violence.

The incendiaries, who were a gang of laborers, having escaped or
mingled with the crowd there was nothing for the force to do. Inspec-

tor FOLK remained with them in the vicinity, however, until 3 A. M. of the next morning, when they were dismissed to their several precincts.

On Thursday and Friday the force was kept in constant readiness, but their services were not needed, and on the latter day they were dismissed to their usual duties.

It is well known that Inspector FOLK is a man of lion heart, never knowing what fear is; fertile in emergencies, and always in the advance where there is danger. His long experience as Chief of Police, and subsequently as Inspector, together with the characteristics mentioned, secured for him the confidence of "all Brooklyn," and the military and civil authorities were at his disposal. There was great trepidation in Brooklyn when he left, and feeling of security when he returned. His headquarters were at the City Hall, and from the Sheriff, Mayor, and military authorities, he was tendered all the co-operation he could desire. His force—Capt. POWERS, of the Forty-fourth Precinct, a most valuable officer, being in command under him—were faithful, willing and constant to a man; he cannot designate one who failed in the entire and cheerful discharge of duty.

To Inspector FOLK's excellent disposition of the small force at his command, to the prestige that his determined character had won, and his constant vigilance, Brooklyn owes its immunity from burning, sacking, pillage, and carnage, such as characterized its neighbor across the water.

The most valuable aid to the promptness and efficiency of the action of the Commissioners and force during Riot Week was the

TELEGRAPH BUREAU,

composed of the following gentlemen : JAMES CROWLEY, Superintendent; ELDRED POLHAMUS, Deputy Superintendent; Messrs. CHAS. L. CHAPIN, JOHN A. K. DUVALL, and JAMES A. LUCAS, Operators.

This Bureau is considered the right arm of the Police Department, and certainly, during Riot Week, more than justified the estimation. The movements of the force, and of the military operating with them, were mainly guided by means of it, and too much credit cannot be awarded to those connected with the Bureau who devoted themselves so constantly to its laborious duties. Messrs. CROWLEY, POLHAMUS, DUVALL, and LUCAS were, for four days and nights, constantly occupied, faithful and laborious, the latter only yielding when he was taken home • vi et armis, by order of the Commissioners, because of being too ill to safely remain at his post; Mr. CHAPIN also shared in the duties.

There are thirty-two telegraphic stations in the city, all centralizing at headquarters; they are divided into five sections—the north, east, south, west, and central. Some idea of the labor entailed, during the riots, upon the gentlemen named, can be had, when it is stated that in the first four days there were *five thousand three hundred and seven* dispatches received and sent from headquarters; besides this, were a large number of telegraphs from one Precinct to another. The work in this Bureau for the four days exceeded that of the whole of any one mouth preceding. The inestimable value of the telegraph was never better evidenced than on this occasion, and the fidelity and efficiency of those in charge of it never so severely tested and so well proven.

Mr. POLHAMUS was at the office early Monday of the outbreak, and was joined by Mr. CROWLEY about 11 A. M. At 9.20 A. M. the mob had cut down the poles on Third Avenue, and thus destroyed the wires in the north section, interrupting communication with the Precincts at Fort Washington, Manhattanville, Harlem, Yorkville, and Blooming-dale, as also with the Nineteenth Precinct. Fortunately, however, at an earlier hour, the operators had sent all necessary word to these Pre-cincts, so that the forces therefrom acted intelligently and without fur-ther instruction. The rioters also cut down the poles in the First Ave-nue, between the Seventeenth and Eighteenth Precincts, and destroyed the wires in Twenty-second Street, in the vicinity of First, Second, and Third Avenues. Another mob cut down the poles in Ninth Avenue, be-tween the Twentieth and Twenty-second Precincts.

This was the state of affairs with the telegraph on Monday evening, and Messrs. CROWLEY and POLHAMUS started out to repair lines and renew connection. The details of their operations it is not proper to give, but, by dint of disguises, ingenuity, and courage, they succeeded in reconnecting the lines over house-tops, through yards, and across streets, and restoring communication. While engaged in doing this they had repeatedly to mingle with the mob, appear to be part and parcel of them, and run a hazard which none but bold men, bent on a thorough discharge of duty, would have incurred. By Tuesday morning the work was com-pleted in the north section, and by Wednesday evening they had the entire line in working order again.

The rioters had cut down over sixty poles, using broadaxes, and leveling them close to the sidewalk; six were cut down on the Third Avenue, thirty on the First, a number on Twenty-second Street, and twenty-four on Ninth Avenue; upwards of twelve miles of wire was rendered useless. When it is remembered that Messrs. CROWLEY and POLHAMUS restored the line without the aid of a pole, and without being detected by the mob, though often in their midst and always in their immediate vicinity, the amount of their labor and the caution, ingenuity, and courage required can be estimated.

The duty of these repairs, however, was not the only ones they were called on to perform, for it was their's also to accompany the police on sundry expeditions, and be prepared to reconstruct any communication which might be interrupted during conflicts or riots arising. The force bear willing testimony not only to their promptness in doing this, but to their readiness in "taking a hand in" when the use of the locust was necessary.

Not a few incidents of interest occurred to Messrs. CROWLEY and POLHAMUS during the four days, and we relate a few of them :

On the Monday of the outbreak Mr. CROWLEY was on his way to town, from Yorkville, where he resides, on the Third Avenue cars. They were interrupted and stopped by the mob, and Mr. CROWLEY unsuspectedly abdicated with others of the passengers. So soon as he got out, he discovered some of the mob cutting down a telegraph pole, and impulsively hastened to prevent them. He was at once pointed out as " A " —we will not say what, but substitute a dash——" operator," and seized; some wanted to "smash him," some to kill him, and various equally pleasant propositions were made for his disposal. Quickly perceiving the state of affairs, he so demeaned himself as to disarm suspicion for a while, at least, and was kept a prisoner for over an hour in the mob, most of the time closely guarded, until, in some exciting demonstration made by them he was for the time forgotten, edged his way out, and betook himself, at a Flora Temple pace, to sections in which he was secure. Had he been known, there is no doubt but that the Bureau to-day would have been without his intelligent and valuable services.

When on an expedition in Roosevelt Street, with the police and military, Mr. POLHAMUS had his boots burned off while working his way over the burning timbers of the fires, there, in order to discover the injury, if any, done to the wires. Here, too, himself and Mr. CROWLEY, both of whom were in citizen's dress, came near being clubbed to death by the police of the Seventeenth Ward, who took them for rioters, because of their eager movements, and they were saved by the timely interference of Capt. BROWER.

It is a noticeable fact that the rioters, in their operations on the telegraph, were destroying that which finds a large portion of its duty in restoring to them their lost children, wandering wives, sons, and brothers. During the evening that preceded the destruction, some thirteen of these were restored or their whereabouts reported.

On Monday night Mr. POLHAMUS accompanied Inspector CARPENTER to the *Tribune* Buildings, where such an exemplary punishment was administed to the mob. One of the force was shot while by his side, Mr. P. narrowly escaping the ball.

Mr. CROWLEY, on hearing that the wires in the Ninth and Tenth

Avenues had been destroyed, hastened to repair them. On reaching the vicinity and seeing there a large mob, he hesitated, very properly, to go among it; but seeing a carriage driving in its direction, in which was a well and justly-beloved Catholic priest, a good man and Christian, with whom he was acquainted, he hailed him and was taken in. On reaching Forty-second Street and Tenth Avenue the mob surrounded the carriage and its inmates, and, imagining (from their moral and exemplary appearance) that they were reporters, cried, " Down with the d—d reporters!" &c., &c. Matters looked threatening enough until the good man—we refer now to the priest—made himself recognized, and under his recognition Mr. CROWLEY escaped.

On several occasions Messrs. CROWLEY and POLHAMUS took a hack and acted as its drivers, both seated on the box. Thus they visited the infected districts frequently, and brought back to headquarters valuable information. On one occasion, however, these amateur Jehus found themselves in a predicament. They had been up the Third Avenue, and were returning; had reached Houston Street, and were hailed by some five of a prowling gang, who demanded that they should drive them down town. The Jehus were unarmed, and compliance was the better part of valor; the route was along Houston Street, too, and once Mulberry Street reached, the drivers were all safe and the inmates prisoners. So " Get in, boys!" was the response. They had not driven far, however, before a counter drive was ordered, and, under indications of some four or five pistols, was complied with. Reaching an ale-house in the Tenth Ward, the party got out, declared CROWLEY and POLHAMUS to be " good boys," and not only entertained them with lemonade, but paid them fifty cents for the compulsory drive. The one was drank, the other received, and they left,—the party of outlaws impressed with the belief that they were as jolly and good-natured drivers as hack-stands can boast of. This occurred at 4½ o'clock Wednesday morning.

On Tuesday morning, at three o'clock, Messrs. CROWLEY and POLHAMUS were coming down Third Avenue in a carriage. They passed Eighty-sixth Street and did not see a soul stirring; before reaching Seventy-seventh Street the store on the corner of Eighty-sixth Street and the avenue was a mass of flames. The rioters and thieves must have been at work as they drove by.

While making an examination of the wires in the Second Avenue, Mr. CROWLEY was suspected by the mob, set upon, and only escaped severe usage by mingling in with them, and, to all appearances, being as ready for lawlessness and spoils as they.

On the many trips of himself and Mr. POLHAMUS, their wagons broke down twice,—once in the immediate vicinity of a First-Avenue mob. They were soon surrounded, and would have been killed had their identity been established. A plausible story of being Westchester farmers saved them, though a demand for money was not complied with.

Among the obligations due from our citizens for the prompt suppression of the riot and their exemption from unprecedented excesses, those to the gentlemen named in this article are not the least. They proved themselves, those in the office and those whose duties called them from it, the former faithful, constant, unwearying, and the latter energetic and courageous,—accomplishing, through perils which few would voluntarily encounter, a work which, for the well-being of the city, was of the greatest importance.

An invaluable portion of the Metropolitan Police at all times, and especially in such emergencies as arose during Riot Week, is the

DETECTIVE FORCE,

which is organized with JOHN YOUNG as Chief; M. B. MORSE, Clerk; and the following force : Messrs. BENNETT, McCORD, FARLEY, ROACH, RADFORD, SMITH, SLOWEY, DUSENBURY, MACDOUGAL, ELDER, EUSTACE, WILSON, KELSO, TIEMAN, and KEEFE.

The requirements for a Detective are more than ordinary intelligence, shrewdness, and sagacity, and an unfailing supply of courage. The work performed by the force named, more than sustained any claims that might be made for the possession of these qualifications.

Those of this force living up town had early indications of the riots. They mingled with the mob, ascertained their feelings and purposes, and, on this information, hastened to headquarters, giving information, on which many prompt, intelligent and effective movements were based.

The operations of this Department can only be spoken of generally, as it would be adverse to its efficiency to detail the many moves adopted by its members to perfect the duties upon which they were sent. But during the riots they were incessantly occupied, night and day, getting for four days and nights no rest, and being constantly on secret service or acting as scouts and guides for the military and police in their different dispositions. Chief YOUNG, in reviewing the conduct of each individual member of his command, cannot name one who did not discharge his duty thoroughly, faithfully, and courageously. It must be remembered that it was theirs to go into the infected districts, penetrate to the very heart of the mob, and be where identification would have been followed by a horrible death. They went disguised in all ways, now as laborers and again as rioters, sometimes on horseback, sometimes driving hacks and carts, and often were part and parcel of the lawless. On several occasions the members of the force were suspected as " KENNEDY'S spies," and nothing but a bold front, earnest denial, and prompt co-operation with the mob, saved their lives. On many occasions, while walking through the riotous crowds, they would evade suspicion by going, as though on business, to dwellings, ringing the bells and entering. On getting inside they explained the exigency and waited there till it had passed.

The designed movements of the rioters toward the lower portion of the city were ascertained by the detectives, and the prompt information brought to headquarters enabled the Commissioners to meet and defeat them.

Detective SLOWEY was the only one of the force injured. He was in the heart of the riotous district on the Second Avenue, and was identified and set upon. He made good fight, but was knocked down and badly beaten; regaining his feet he managed to get on to the steps of a house, where he kept the gang at bay until the courageous lady occupying it opened the door and admitted him. He remained here until his howling assailants left and then again started on duty.

The telegraph communications, as we have heretofore stated, were cut off in several directions, and the Detectives had to convey the many messages which the destruction interrupted. This duty involved the greatest risk of life, but was always promptly and successfully performed.

During the sacking and burning of the different premises, portions of the Detectives were present, and, "spotting" the ringleaders would follow them afterward for hours, until they separated from their associates, and then pouncing upon them would run them into the nearest station-house. Thus many important arrests were made.

On and after Tuesday, when the rioters took the shape of thieves, the detective force made visits to the different "Lushing Cribs" in Eighth and Fourteenth Streets, some six places in all, and arrested about thirty noted burglars, thieves, and garroters, of this and other cities, who were on hand to reap a harvest. The rascals were locked up until the excitement was over, and by this much property was saved.

At the fight at Pitt and Broome Streets, between the military and rioters, where the latter were so fearfully slaughtered, the Detectives were prominent, having notified headquarters of the mob and acted as guides for the military. It was the scene of the most exemplary punishment the mob during the four days received. But for the Detectives and their promptness on that occasion, there would have been riot and pillage in the very heart of the city. The mob which made the first attack on the Mayor's house, Fifth Avenue, was also accompanied by the Detectives, and word was conveyed by them to headquarters, which secured for the rioters the reception they had at Broadway and Amity Street by Inspector CARPENTER and his command. In this fight the Detectives—only three were together at any time—took a hand and did great execution.

During the riots this force was also occupied in giving information to the negroes in quarters threatened by the mob, and directing them where to find safety, in escorting citizens home through the infected districts, and in fact were ubiquitous and ever at work. One duty performed was visiting the different forts in the vicinity, and conveying orders to those in command of the forces there. After the riots were over the duty of the force did not cease, for they were engaged in discovering the whereabouts of the stolen goods, and in this their services have been of the utmost value, and by them an immense amount of property has been recovered.

Although the Detective force was not in many of the fights, its duties, as will readily be seen, were of the most important, constant, and perilous character. It has covered itself with honor, and our citizens will recognize in it one of the most valuable, faithful, and effective protectives to the peace of the city and individual security. Only numbering fifteen, yet this force accomplished, successfully and bravely, an amount of work of which the mention made gives but a glimpse.

Chief YOUNG, who was busily engaged at headquarters during the riot, beside the direction of his command had the additional labor of "Commissary of Subsistence" for the police, military, specials, and refugees concentrated there. There were unitedly over 5,000 to be fed daily; and so well did he manage that not one but who had an abundance of everything, and all of the best, without confusion or discomfort. Some 50,000 gallons of coffee were furnished during his commissaryship, and he mentions as an interesting fact that, among the thousands congregating at headquarters, not a single case occurred where a party was under the influence of liquor. Chief YOUNG attributes this to the ever-ready and liberal supply of coffee, which was eagerly taken in preference to all other stimulants. He was efficiently aided, during the arduous days and nights, in this new branch of business, by Sergeant LEFFERTS and assistants, of the Fourth District Court, and Officer WEBB, of the Superintendent's Office, both of whom were unwearying.

The record of the Detective force affords no very thrilling incidents, notwithstanding theirs were duties of constant hazard and of vital importance to the public. Chief YOUNG, whose fitness for his position has been fully manifested, intelligently directed their movements. He has fully proven his capacity for the important position he holds, and the detectives, guided by his intelligent and cool judgment, have made for themselves an honorable prominence and reputation.

It is now proposed to speak of the several precincts, and the duties performed by the forces thereof. From the details there will be an opportunity of judging of the amount of labor performed, and the fidelity which characterized the performance. The precincts will be taken in their numerical order :

First Precinct.

Jacob B. Warlow, Captain, No. 29 Broad Street. On the morning of Monday of Riot Week Capt. Warlow was ordered with his command to headquarters. He at once sent there one section under Roundsman Connor, which participated in the defeat of the mob, in the afternoon, at Broadway and Amity Street. His entire command reported at headquarters toward evening, and were ordered on duty at the City Hall. Here about 8 o'clock Capt. Warlow received word that there was a riot in his own district and orders to quell it. Sergts. Cherry and McCleary started in advance of the force, and meeting a body of rioters in New Street were attacked, stoned, and badly beaten before Capt. Warlow and force could come to their rescue, they having *en route* been detained by a demonstration made upon Downing's saloon, Broad Street. When the force did reach them, short work was made of the assailants. The command then repaired to its station-house, where a dispatch to proceed to the *Tribune* Buildings was received; instantly off on double-quick, on reaching Nassau and Spruce Streets a charge was made upon the mob, which had already sacked and were setting fire to the office, and it was driven in all directions. During this attack upon the mob Officer Welling was shot in the right shoulder. The force remained in charge of the building till 10 P. M., when ordered to headquarters, and were on duty there all night.

Tuesday the First Precinct force were a portion of Inspector Carpenter's command on the visit to the Second Avenue, and participated in the duties and dangers of that hazardous tour. On return to headquarters, were again sent to the City Hall. At 2 P. M. thirty men were sent, under Sergeant Matthew, to report for duty to Capt. Bryan, of the Fourth Precinct, and subsequently assisted in repelling the attack on Brooks Brothers' clothing store; this force remained in the Fourth Precinct until Saturday, pretty constantly engaged in dispersing crowds and saving persons and property. The balance of the force on Wednesday had permanently returned to its own precinct.

Capt. WARLOW awards to his men the highest praise as prompt, willing, courageous. Sergt. BABCOCK, who was absent, on hearing of the riot, returned and reported for duty before expiration of leave.

On the morning of the 14th, in Second Avenue, the fighting was very severe, gun and pistol shots and missiles of all kinds being hurled from the buildings on to the police. In the charge ordered by Inspector CARPENTER into the houses, up and on to their roofs, the First Precinct were prominent. To reach the rioters overhead was a perilous task; the scuttles were narrow; six determined men could have kept five hundred at bay; but a portion of the force made a rush, and soon gained the roofs, where a hand-to-hand conflict ensued; in every instance the rioters were knocked senseless; others searched the rooms. Rioters in their fright dropped from second and third story windows, some escaping unharmed, others receiving fearful injuries.

Four of the rioters fled into a yard, and took shelter in an out-house. They were well armed, and how to get them out was the question. Assailing their shelter would be certain death. At length an ingenious plan was adopted to dislodge them. A large coping-stone, from the roof of the house overtopping it, was dropped on the out-house, demolishing one side and uncovering the refugees, who on the instant were assailed by the police in waiting, and rendered powerless for good or evil. During this exciting and terrible fight Capt. WARLOW was struck on the foot with a stone, and two of his toes mashed badly, but he continued, thus crippled, on duty.

On the evening of the 14th, when BROOKS BROTHERS' clothing store was attacked, and thirty of this precinct served in its defence, all the street lamps in the vicinity were turned out, and the lights in all the adjacent houses were extinguished. The night was very dark. The charge of the police upon the mob was met by a volley of musketry, stones, bricks, &c., from all directions. BROOKS BROTHERS' store had been lighted up by the rioters so as to enable them to select and carry off the most valuable of the goods. When in front of the building, Sergt. MATTHEW, with his men, of the First Precinct, charged into the store, and attacked the rioters. Then commenced a scene which is indescribable. The thieves attempted to rush through the police and escape. Some fell upon their knees before the uplifted clubs, shrieking for mercy, while the others wildly rushed in search of ways for safe exit. On the second story, however, the rioters showed fight; but the police, making a determined charge, soon drove them into the rear building, where the majority of them, with most of their spoils, were kept, and ultimately secured.

The appearance of the officers was hailed with terror by most of the lawless. Some jumped down stairs at one leap, while others were saved

3

the trouble of a similar agile performance by the application of the locust. Those rioters who were driven outside the building were attended to by the reserves of the Third and Fourth Precincts, who drove them, with terrible punishment, down Catharine and through Cherry Street.

Officer VAN RANST, of the First Precinct, received a pistol ball in his cap, where it lodged, and was found by him the next morning. Had he been but a little taller the bullet would have pierced his brain.

At the time the Sergeants were beaten in New Street, Mr. CHERRY had a negro under his protection, whom he ultimately succeeded in saving.

One of the rioters, a tall, powerful fellow, at BROOKS BROTHERS' store, made savage fight. Two of the police of the First Precinct found it necessary for their own safety to quiet him. It was the alternative of their lives or his. He had loaded himself with plunder, and only dropped it to make fight with them.

After the force of the First Precinct had been returned to their station-house, they were engaged in recovering stolen goods, visiting the tenement houses in Cherry and Market Streets, and recovered several wagon loads of property.

The record of this precinct is an honorable one, and the Captain, his officers, and men never once failed in an entire and thorough discharge of their duty.

Second Precinct.

On Monday the force of the Second Precinct, No. 49 Beekman Street, Capt. SQUIRES, were kept in the ward because of the many riotous demonstrations at and around Printing-house Square.

The beginning of the disturbances in this precinct was in South Street, where a gang attacked a negro sailor. He was rescued by Officers WATERS and GILLEN, after much difficulty; who also arrested several of his assailants. All the hotels and restaurants in that section having colored help were threatened, and by noon a large crowd had gathered in Park Row. Every car and omnibus was searched for colored people, and any discovered were set upon and beaten. The whole force were engaged in preventing these assaults. Sergeant CORNWELL, with a section of men, was active in rescuing the unfortunate victims, and, with his force, was the means of saving many from savage, and probably fatal, usage. In this duty they incurred the jeers and abuse of the mob, but had no collision.

During the absence of the force, Sergeant ESTERBROOK, with one man, was left in charge of the station. A number of colored people had fled to it for protection, and the mob paid it a visit, intending to seize them and fire the building. The Sergeant and his aid boldly met them, threatening to shoot the first one who attempted to enter. Their bold front kept the mob at bay until reinforcements arrived, before whom the rioters scattered. In the afternoon Sergeant KELLY, with a platoon of men, dispersed gatherings in the Park. In the evening a portion of the force patrolled the precinct, the balance being held in reserve at the sta. tion. Sergeant SNODGRASS, in citizen's dress, mingled among the mob at the *Tribune* Buildings, and ascertaining that the design was to fire it, hurried back to the station, and, in command of the reserve, returned to the scene, joining in the successful assault upon the mob. Sergeants Es- TERBROOK and CORNWELL also participated in this, Sergeant KELLY re- maining in charge of the precinct. Much hard patrol duty was done by the force the balance of the night.

During the evening one section, under Sergeant SNODGRASS, was transferred to headquarters, and, on Tuesday, participated in the attack by Inspector CARPENTER's command upon the houses in Second Avenue, near Twenty-second Street, and in the subsequent encounters in that sec- tion. On the occasion of the storming of the houses, Officers WATSON and COLE entered into rivalry to see who would first reach the roof of a building from which the rioters had been especially annoying. They reached the scuttle together, but it being only large enough to pass one at a time, WATSON edged through and won the first honors. He was forthwith attacked by a rioter armed with a bar of iron, who made a lunge at his head; he dodged and escaped, but so violently had the fel- low struck, that on missing his mark he lost his balance, and would have fallen to the street but for a blow from WATSON's club, which knocked him back and sent him reeling down upon the roof. Officer COLE, al- though behind WATSON on the roof, was not a whit behind him, when there, in courage and execution. He was instantly encountered by the rioters, but his courage and coolness stood him well in hand. All the force of this precinct present on this occasion were actively engaged and exhibited the utmost courage.

On return to headquarters, the platoon was transferred to Capt. LORD's command, on guard duty, where it remained, doing valuable duty, until Saturday, when it was ordered to its own quarters.

Besides the services mentioned, one section of this precinct was detailed for duty on the river, which was vigilantly performed.

On Monday, Sergt. SNODGRASS notified headquarters of an intended attack on the Fifth-avenue Hotel—getting his information from the mob up Broadway. It was thus anticipated and prevented.

The officers and men of this precinct did thoroughly all they were

called upon to do, and there was no instance of hesitancy or want of
nerve among them.

Third Precinct.

The force of the Third Precinct, No. 160 Chambers Street, Capt.
GREER, repaired, at 5 P. M. on Monday, to headquarters, Sergts. FINNEY,
ROBINSON, and WEBB accompanying; at 6 P. M., with Inspector CAR-
PENTER's command, marched to the Park, and took a hand in the punish-
ment of the rioters who were fleeing after their defeat at the *Tribune*
Buildings. On the same evening they were with Inspector CARPENTER in
the tour through the Fourth Ward, thence proceeding to headquarters,
where they were held in reserve all night.

On Tuesday, on duty with Inspector CARPENTER's command in the
hazardous visit to Second Avenue and tour through the infected vicinity
thereof, and then were ordered to Inspector LEONARD's command at the
City Hall. Sergt. FINNEY, with twenty-five of the force, was sent by the
Inspector to Capt. BRYAN, of the Fourth, to assist in suppressing the riot
at BROOKS BROTHERS' clothing store. This done, and they returned, the
whole force being held in reserve at the City Hall until Wednesday
night. Meantime, however, detachments were constantly being sent on
duty; in the afternoon, to protect STUART's sugar refinery, at Chambers
and Greenwich Streets; then to suppress a disturbance at Pier No. 4,
North River, which they did, dispersing the rioters; and again to the refinery.

Each duty was well performed; numerous growing disturbances
were checked. From Thursday morning the force was held in reserve
at its own station until Saturday, when it resumed ordinary patrol duty;
meantime, however, Capt. GREER had been keeping scouting parties out,
who thoroughly worked the entire precinct.

During the tour through the Fourth Ward Sergeant ROBINSON was
attacked by a tall, powerful fellow, who aimed a blow at his head with a
cooper's adze. He evaded this, and with a well directed return from his
club knocked the rascal senseless.

At the assault on the houses on Second Avenue, from which the
rioters had been firing and hurling missiles, Sergeant ROBINSON called
on the men of the Third to follow him, and charged upon a porter-house
from which much injury had been inflicted. He was followed by Sergeant FINNEY, Roundsman FARRELL, and others, forced an entrance; drove
the gang inside up on to the roof or out of the windows. One escaped
by jumping from the second-story window; another fell from the roof

and was badly injured. The house was speedily cleared and all who could be got hold of were severely punished.

It was about this time that Col. O'BRIEN came up with his command, the police giving him the front. He unlimbered his pieces, notified the mob in the street to disperse, and after waiting for them to do so a sufficient time, fired; he had elevated his guns so as to shoot over the heads of the crowd, giving as his reason that he did not want to hurt them if scaring would do as well. He was fiendishly murdered soon after.

When ordered to aid in saving BROOKS BROTHERS' store, Sergt. FINNEY took his men all the way on the double-quick. After reaching there, upwards of a hundred shots were fired by the rioters; Sergt. FINNEY was wounded in the face, and Roundsman FARRELL took command during the balance of the conflict, which was short and decisive, the Third doing bravely. Roundsman FARRELL (it was a close fight at BROOKS') broke his club on the first blow, and then used his pistol. Many of the rioters, finding themselves beaten, fell on their knees and begged for mercy; others jumped from the lower floors of the store, and others rushed against locked and barred doors, hoping to burst them open and escape. They paid heavily for that night's transgression.

The force, after this duty, were returned to the City Hall at 10 P. M. Sergt. ROBINSON was ordered by Inspector LEONARD to take charge of Printing-house Square, which he did, with fifteen men of his precinct. All was quiet there until two o'clock A. M. of Tuesday, when a gang of rioters appeared, and threatened the *Times* and *Tribune* Buildings. A banner carried by them was inscribed, "We'll hang old GREELEY on a sour-apple tree," and this line they were singing. Before they could know who assailed them Sergt. ROBINSON, with his little force, made a charge and gave them a shower of locust. They fled, feeling, if not singing, a different tune from the one to which they had adapted the line quoted.

An hour later, Sergt. ROBINSON detected a man prowling around the *Tribune* office; questions only begot from him evasive answers; he was arrested, searched, and a revolver, full-cocked, with two barrels discharged, found on him. He proved to be JAMES FITZGERRON, was locked up, and next morning committed in default of $500 bail.

The scouting parties sent out by Capt. GREER were of great service in his precinct—during the period of the excitement all acts of pillage being prevented.

On Thursday, at 5 P. M., while Sergt. ROBINSON was at the Hudson River depot, a colored woman, with a babe in her arms, came up and begged protection. He said she should have it, and meantime two more colored women and three more children appealed to him. He conducted them to the station-house, where Capt. GREER gave them shelter and food; they had been without food, and hiding here and there, for over forty-eight hours.

On Saturday, 18th, at 6 P. M., Sergt. ROBINSON and a section of men were ordered to the Central Office on special duty. At 4 A. M. on Sunday, they were ordered to join the command of Capt. DIXON, of the Twenty-eighth Precinct, which embarked at the foot of Canal Street for a visit to different towns on the Hudson, where trouble was antici-pated. Hastings, Tarrytown, Sing Sing, and Peekskill were visited; at each place the men disembarked and made reconnoissance. On the re-turn from Peekskill all these places were again visited. The command returned to this city on the following evening.

On Wednesday, at 4 A. M., Sergeant ROBINSON, with seven men, formed another command, under Capt. DIXON, on an expedition to Sta-ten Island. They landed at Port Richmond, from thence proceeded to New Brighton, and then across to Quarantine. Here Capt. DIXON heard of a disturbance near Wood Road, where a day before two soldiers had been killed. He repaired at once to Vanderbilt Landing, was refused the co-operation of some military there, but proceeded, with his small force, to and through the whole district where the trouble had occurred. About 3 P. M. the force returned to the city, and were met at Canal Street by a company of the Seventh Regiment who were in waiting to accompany them to Flushing. Off they started again, arriving there at 8 P. M., when a thorough tour of the place was made. The force quar-tered on the boat that night, a guard being left on duty. Next morn-ing again patrolled the village and vicinity, and at 11 A. M. returned to New York, when the expedition was dismissed, each squad being or-dered to its precinct.

It will be admitted that the force of the Third Precinct were kept pretty constantly engaged, abroad as well as at home; and their duties, constant and arduous as they were, were most faithfully and willingly performed.

Fourth Precinct.

Monday afternoon, a portion of the force of the Fourth Precinct—Captain BRYAN, No. 9 Oak Street—reported at headquarters, under Ser-geants DELANY and LOCKWOOD,—only one section being retained at the station, under Sergeants RODE and WILLIAMS, the former in command. This was engaged all day in saving the lives of colored persons in the precinct, some seventy of whom were rescued from gangs, and brought for safety to the station-house. Roundsman WEBB was unwearying and most faithful in discharge of this duty.   During the day, thirteen houses occupied by this class were sacked and partially burned, the active efforts of the force preventing their entire destruction.   In the evening, Sergeant WILLIAMS and Roundsman WEBB, with four men, all in citizen's dress, mingled with the crowd at the *Tribune* Buildings, and, ascertaining its purpose, made prompt report to Captain BRYAN, who, with what men he had, was soon thereafter engaged, with the Twenty-sixth Precinct, in the defeat of the mob.   Subsequently Captain BRYAN acted as guide on Inspector CARPENTER's tour through the Fourth Ward, and, with some of his precinct, joined in the attacks upon the mob in Roosevelt and in Dover Streets.   During all Monday night, and until Tuesday morning, the second section were constantly on active duty in the ward.

On the evening of Monday, an attack was made on the station-house. Sergeant RODE was in command, with only eight men in the house at the time.   The mob numbered some five or six hundred.   With two unloaded muskets, eight men, and a bold front, the rioters were so frightened that they fled on the first demonstration of the command.

In Roosevelt Street Sergeant RODE, while alone, saw a mob collected and a man attempting to batter in the door of a Mrs. JOHNSON's house, who owns houses in the Fourth Ward, and rents them to negroes.   He immediately seized the man, and a struggle ensued; the Sergeant, however, clung to him until the fellow received aid and the officer was overpowered by superior numbers.   He was compelled to let him go, but it was not before all the clothing had been torn from the body of the rioter. As soon as the man was rescued the mob commenced stoning the Sergeant, and a brick striking him on the chest, disabled him.   Fortunately, at this juncture, Sergeant DELANY, with a platoon of men, arrived, rescued the Sergeant, and put the rioters to flight.

On Tuesday, the balance of the force of the precinct were returned to the station.   They had been doing good duty ; were in the first battle of the campaign, under Inspector CARPENTER, at Broadway and Amity ; at midnight, Monday, were with the force which recovered the body of the negro hung in Clarkson Street; and on Tuesday, with Inspector DILK's command, were in the fierce fight at Second Avenue and Twenty-first Street.   About noon GODFREY's gun store was attacked, and its pillage prevented by Sergeant RODE.   At dusk scouting parties were sent out.   Patrolmen PLOTT, KENNEDY, and DAVIS were among the mob gathering at BROOKS & BROTHERS' store in Catharine Street, were recognized, attacked, and very badly beaten.   They were brought to the station-house by a party of citizens.   The entire force repaired to the store, made battle with, and dispersed, the mob.   Had not broken ranks on return ere word came of the sacking of a boot and shoe store in Catharine Street; repaired on the double-quick, had a sharp fight, and cleared the streets; counter-marched down Catharine Street, halting 400 feet from Brooks & Brothers' store, where the mob had reassembled, busy in plundering.   Captain Bryan went forward, and ascertaining the work going on, returned to his command and ordered a charge, which was made in gallant style.   Some hundreds, it is estimated, of the rioters and thieves, were badly beaten in this charge.   The street and store were cleared, and a portion of the force remained in charge of the building until relieved by the Seventh Precinct.   Until Wednesday morning, scouting parties were sent in all parts of the precinct.   Sergeant Rode and Officer Irvin came upon a gang attempting to break into Lord & Taylor's store, from Catharine Street; they fled, but received a discharge from revolvers, unfortunately without injury.

At the riot at Brooks', Sergeant Delany was fired at by a man who was only about four feet from him, the wadding of the pistol knocking the Sergeant's cap off.

There were no further disturbances in this precinct, and, until Friday, the force were engaged in hunting up goods stolen from Brooks Brothers' recovering some $5,000 worth stowed away in different houses in the ward.

On Saturday, regular patrol duty was resumed.   All of Captain Bryan's men had seen constant duty, laboriously and most faithfully performed.   They responded to every call with alacrity, and evinced unflinching courage.

Fifth Precinct.

At noon on Monday, a portion of the force of the Fifth Precinct, Captain Petty, No. 49 Leonard Street, reported under Roundsman Hessian at headquarters—the rest held in reserve for ward duty. In the afternoon Captain Petty, who visited Thomas Street alone and in citizen's dress, met a crowd in an alleyway, battering in the doors of houses occupied by colored people. He interposed, and was at once assailed by divers missiles; his chances of being stoned to death were increasing when some of the reserve came to his rescue, and drove off the rioters, clearing that vicinity of them.

In the evening, the balance of the force reported at headquarters, whence, at about 11 P. M., under Captain Petty, they joined Inspector Leonard's command, which marched to the City Hall. From here they were engaged in the various expeditions in the lower sections of the city until Tuesday A. M., when ordered to headquarters. Captain Petty with 200 men (including his own precinct force) was soon after ordered to the protection of the soap factory in Sixteenth Street, between Eighth and Ninth Avenues. When the force came in sight, two blocks off, the mob, which Captain Petty characterizes as the most pusillanimous he ever saw, fled in all directions; chase was given them, but in vain. Four employees were found in the factory, who had been bravely and successfully defending it. The force marched through Eighth and Ninth Avenues and the intersecting streets as far as Nineteenth Street, clearing the entire section of all gatherings, and returning to headquarters, having fully accomplished its purpose. In the afternoon, Captain Petty and his men were a portion of Captain Helm's command in the encounters with the mob at the Second Avenue wire factory, where some thousands of carbines were stored, and which the mob were pillaging. A severe battle was had here; and a charge into the factory, filled with rioters, was ordered. Captain Petty, with ten of his men, made their way to the fifth floor, where many of the rioters were caught. Some went down the hatchway, some ran the gauntlet of the police on the stairs, but all were more or less punished. At one time eight of them lay blocking up a doorway. After securing a large number of arms, and loading them into a wagon, the entire command of Captain Helm reformed on the avenue, only to find themselves hemmed in on all sides by an excited and threatening crowd, overpowering in numbers. They were relieved from their critical position—one from which they could not have escaped without great loss of life—by the opportune arrival of Inspector Dilks and his command, with whom, the Fifth acting as escort to the wagon load of carbines, they returned to headquarters.

On Wednesday morning, Captain Petty, in command of a company of military and a body of specials, made a tour through the infected districts of the First and Second Avenues, but found all quiet save the women, who, on the advent of the force, fearing a repetition of the exemplary punishment the rioters had received during the day, made the usually quiet hours ring with their shrieks and screams. The force were on this tour for three hours. During Wednesday the Fifth were on duty at headquarters, and in the evening were returned to their own precinct. From here twenty-five were sent to the Eighth Precinct, under command of Sergeant Brooks, where they remained till Thursday night. The balance kept on patrol and scouting duty until Friday, when the force resumed regular duty.

Officer Field, on Monday and Tuesday, remained in the precinct, on detective duty; he knew, and was known by, all the riotous parties, and was invaluable in prevention of outrages in Thomas, Leonard, and York Streets.

On the morning of the outbreak, the telegraph wires connecting with this station were out of order, and about the first intimation Captain

PETTY received of disturbances was from a terrified colored man, who drove up to the station-house at a racing speed, jumped from his cart, and gave it in charge of the police; he said he was afraid to remain on it, having been pursued by a mob, and only escaping by putting his horse to its speed. He was, with his property, afforded protection.

On Tuesday, attempts were made to organize a mob in the precinct and attack the station-house. Sergeant HIGGINS and Doorman PALLISTER were the only ones there. Some 400 colored persons had taken refuge in the station; these were given weapons, and promised to fight to the last. The doors were barricaded, and the two officers made all preparations to give their assailants a warm reception. About 10 P. M. the mob assembled in front, fired at the building, and were about to fire it, when Inspector CARPENTER, with his command, made their appearance, came on to the mob with a rush, and drove them in all directions. Some time after the Inspector left another demonstration was made, but a company of military, quartered in Worth Street, hurried to the rescue and the mob again fled.

For three days and nights none of the Fifth Precinct had any rest; their duties were numerous and fatiguing, but were performed cheerfully and creditably.

Sixth Precinct.

This precinct, Capt. JOHN JOURDAN, No. 9 Franklin Street, had no little work to do. At 3 P. M. on Monday an attack was made by a large mob on premises of colored people at No. 42 Baxter Street. Capt. JOURDAN, with Sergeants WALSH and McGIVEN and the second platoon, were soon at the spot, and after a severe fight, in which the force was boldly opposed, the rioters were dispersed, many of them badly injured. Of the force, Roundsman RYAN was the only one hurt; he was knocked down and his club wrenched from him, but was at once on his feet again and in the thickest of the fray. Soon after, the Captain, with same officers and platoon, repaired to CROOK's, No. 74 Chatham Street, which was being assailed by a mob. A charge was made unexpectedly upon the rascals, the locust liberally used, and a general scattering ensued. At 5½ P. M. some three hundred men, women, and boys attacked the dwellings of colored people in Pell, near Mott, Street; with the same officers and force, the Captain repaired thither, charged upon and routed the assailants. In this cowardly attack by the rioters, Elizabeth Hennesy, a colored woman, 57 years of age, was struck and severely injured by a brick; she was rescued by the police, and conveyed to the City Hospital. At 6 P. M. upwards of six hundred rioters attacked a house at Leonard and Baxter Streets, occupied by some twenty colored families, stoning in the windows, attempting to break in and fire it. Capt. JOURDAN, with Sergeants WALSH, QUINN, and KENNEDY, and first and second platoons, was speedily on hand; a severe fight ensued; the rioters were effectively handled, and dozens lay senseless on the street; ultimately they fled.

About this time the whole force were ordered to report at headquarters, and while on their way were met at Mott and Grand Streets by a large mob, who greeted them with howling and hooting. They marched steadily on, not noticing the noisy demonstration; but when the crowd assailed them with stones and other missiles, at Broome and Mott Streets, they were wheeled and ordered to a charge, which was made in gallant style and carried with it severe punishment to the rioters, who were soon defeated and—save those who were laying in the street—flying. Roundsman HOPKINS was struck, in this fight, with a stone, on the head, which did him some damage. At 6½ P. M. the force was at headquarters, and soon after were sent with Inspector CARPENTER's command to the Park, where they participated actively—having the right of the line—in punishment meted out to the rioters fleeing from Printing-house Square. After having a settlement with the mob here, Capt. JOURDAN was sent with his force to protect his own ward; came upon a mob of six hundred, attacking Nos. 104 and 105 Park Street, occupied by colored people; made a charge; had to fight hand-to-hand, using locusts effectively; beat and scattered the rioters. This done, Capt. JOURDAN repaired to the station-house, and soon after was ordered to the Fourth Precinct, in conjunction with Capt. BRYAN and his men, to take charge of the Fourth and Sixth Precincts; heard of a riot in Baxter Street, in a locality known as Cow Bay; hurried there, and dispersed a mob which was attacking dwellings; returned to the Fourth Precinct, and during the balance of the night were in reserve.

Tuesday morning a mob in Leonard Street was assaulting and beating colored people. Capt. JOURDAN, with a force, repaired there, defeated and dispersed the mob, rescued six negroes and brought them in safety to the station. At 3 P. M. hundreds of the lawless attacked the negro dwellings in Catharine Lane, near Elm. The Sixth Precinct were promptly to the scene, and prevented injury to person or property.

From this time until Wednesday morning quiet prevailed, until 11 o'clock, when Capt. JOURDAN, Sergts. QUINN and KENNEDY, were engaged in quelling a mob in Centre, near Worth Street, who were assailing every colored person they met. After this, Sergt. WALSH, with half the force, returned to its own precinct.

Early in the evening some four hundred rioters attempted to sack and demolish a building at the corner of Mott and Centre Streets;

Sergt. QUINN, with one platoon, hastened to and attacked the mob. They made a bold resistance, and the fight was severe before they were routed. Here Patrolman CHARLES McDONNELL was injured; he was struck in the face and terribly cut, knocked down, regained his feet, and, despite his condition, rejoined his comrades, and did execution enough to more than compensate for his injuries; he did his part bravely and nobly. During the night (Wednesday) there were many demonstrations against the dwellings Nos. 38 and 40 Baxter Street, occupied by colored people; all of them, however, were promptly met and defeated by the Sixth Precinct, sometimes with and sometimes without a battle.

On Monday the force of this precinct was at times divided; the reserve under Sergeant WALSH was ordered at noon to the aid of Capt. CAMERON, Eighteenth Precinct; they remained there in defence of the station-house until the mob became overwhelming, and were the last of the police who left the building; it was subsequently burned. On Tuesday morning Sergeant WALSH, with one platoon, was part of Inspector CARPENTER's command in the perilous visit to the Second Avenue, where such severe fighting was had. In the afternoon, with his men, he was sent to City Hall, under Inspector LEONARD, where they remained until Wednesday P. M., thence to their own station.

The duties of the officers and men of this precinct, as has been seen, were incessant and arduous; theirs seemed to be an almost continuous series of fights or skirmishes. Not one halted or hesitated; all were brave, all true. Especial praise is awarded to Roundsmen HOPKINS and RYAN, and to Patrolman CHARLES McDONNELL, each of whom on all occasions evinced the greatest courage; the two latter were very roughly handled by the mobs, but never faltered.

On Wednesday evening some four hundred merchants, clerks, and others doing business in Capt. JOURDAN's precinct, tendered their services to him as special patrolmen; they were accepted, sent on duty, and he awards them high praise for the efficiency and value of their services.

Seventh Precinct.

The force of this precinct, Captain THERON R. BENNETT, No. 247 Madison Street, reported at headquarters Monday afternoon, with Sergeants McCONNELL, GARLAND, and CLARK—Sergeant LOUDUN being left in charge of station. The force, with Sergeants McCONNELL and GARLAND, composed a portion of Inspector CARPENTER's command in the attack upon and severe usage of the rioters at Broadway and Amity Street, being active and prominent therein. At night the force reported to Inspector LEONARD, at the City Hall, and was engaged in the many duties which were necessary for the protection of the portion of the city thereabouts. On Tuesday morning they were ordered to headquarters, and subsequently, with Inspector DILKS' command, visited Second Avenue, where the sharp fighting was done, and in which the Seventh were actively engaged. Later in the day, under Inspector LEONARD, a mob at Broadway and Bond Street were attacked and dispersed, the Seventh participating. On return to headquarters, Sergeant McCONNELL relieved Sergeant LOUDON at station, who reported for duty at central office. Captain BENNETT, with his command, was detailed, with a company of military, to visit Thirty-fourth Street, where Colonel O'BRIEN was so horribly murdered, to recover the body. On reaching the ground, it was ascertained that the body had been rescued from the rioters, and taken to Bellevue. On the same evening the force was ordered to the care of its own precinct, where patrol duty was resumed Friday.

On Monday evening Sergeant GARLAND was detached from his command and sent to the Tenth Precinct Station to work the telegraph; about 9 P. M. the building was assailed by a mob, who stoned in the windows; they were fresh from the sacking and destruction of Provost Marshal DUFFY's house. There were but few men in the station, but Surgeon WELLS, and a number of citizens, came to the rescue, the former acting with great coolness and courage. Officer McCLOUD found a small cannon in the building, which was hastily hauled into position at the door, pointed on to the mob, who, at sight of it, broke and scattered. On Tuesday morning Sergeant GARLAND was relieved as telegraph operator, and reported to Inspector DILKS at headquarters, by whom he was detailed as acting adjutant of the battalion of police which the Inspector led to the Second Avenue, as already referred to. He was also in the second expedition to the same section, under Mr. DILKS, and narrowly escaped the ball which came so near cutting off a good man and true in the Inspector, but cut off a tree branch at its bend against him instead. The Sergeant was receiving orders from Mr. D. at the time. In one of the battles with the mob at the Eighteenth Precinct, Sergeant McCONNELL and his command were engaged; they had to enter and clear adjacent houses of parties who were firing from the roofs and windows. The work was well and promptly done, but the street fighting was severe, and the rioters not dispersed until the military, called to the aid of the police, had fired several volleys.

The officers and men of this precinct saw considerable service during the week, and sustained the good repute hitherto attached to them.

Eighth Precinct.

This precinct, Captain M. DE CAMP, No. 127 Wooster Street, was early on active duty. At 9 A. M. Sergeant WADE and ten men reported to Captain SPEIGHT, No 1190 Broadway, Provost Marshal MANIERRE's office, which they assisted in defending. At noon, Sergeant ELLISON, with thirteen men, was sent to protect the Provost Marshal's office at Third Avenue and Forty-sixth Street; on arrival at Third Avenue and Forty-fourth Street he met the provost guard, which had been driven from the Marshal's office, and were fleeing down, pursued by the mob. Checking and reinforcing them, he ordered a wheel, a volley, and a bayonet charge upon the mob; the guard halted, made a move as though about to obey, but finally refused, and, on one of them being knocked down with a stone, they broke and fled. Thus left alone to meet the mob, Sergeant ELLISON and his men, thoughtless of the vast disproportion in numbers, made a desperate charge, and a desperate hand-to-hand fight ensued; the mob stood their ground, fighting fiercely, and finally the force—Sergeant ELLISON badly beaten and in the hands of the rioters —was compelled to fall back in retreat. At this juncture, Sergeant WADE and his men, relieved from duty at No. 1190 Broadway, came on to the ground, hurrying to the relief of their companions, by whom they were greeted with ringing cheers. The mob were threatening to hang ELLISON, and great as was the superiority in numbers, the united force at once charged to the rescue; so impetuous, earnest, and determined was the charge made, so terribly did the locusts do their work, that the mob were forced back some three blocks, fighting all the way, and the Sergeant rescued. But the odds were too great for permanent success; the excited thousands closed in upon the small force from the streets in their rear, pressed back upon them from the front, and they were soon hemmed in; they had to fight their way through and out, contested at every inch of ground, but succeeded, though at a great cost, in extricating themselves from their critical position. In the first of these battles Sergeant ELLISON was badly beaten, taken prisoner, and rescued; Officer VAN BUREN had his leg broken, and Officers CROLIUS, PALMER, and McCAUL were each severely beaten. In the second, Sergeant WADE was hit in the breast with a stone, and the following officers were injured: ANDRE, his head badly cut; LAW, injured in head and body; HART, head and body; BURNS, MERHEF, and MAGERSUPPE, each severely beaten, and heads badly cut. Those who were too badly injured to escape sought refuge in the houses of citizens in the vicinity until they could be removed, and the balance of the force so roughly used, and now scattered, repaired to their station-house, leaving the mob exultant over the defeat of the handful.

Sergeant ELLISON had a sufficiently serious time. When about to fire the gun which he had wrenched from a rioter, it was knocked from his grasp by a brick, going off as it fell and shooting a horse in the leg; he defended himself with a revolver, and, his command being beaten, he retreated, running into a hallway. The mob followed, pulled him out, walked him up and down for awhile, yelling and hooting over his capture, beating him with clubs, and pelting him with stones. Falling from exhaustion, they still continued to beat him. Those who could not get at him dropped large stones over the other's shoulders. At last they left him, thinking him dead, in which condition he lay for twenty or thirty minutes. Two men carried him off towards the Twenty-first Precinct Station. On the way down the mob followed, threatening to attack again, but were driven back by the forces arriving under Sergeant WADE, as before chronicled.

Sergeants WADE and O'CONNOR, with their commands, were at the dispersion of the mob, in the afternoon, on Broadway and Amity Street, and on duty at the City Hall all night. The precinct was joined to Captain WALLING's command on Tuesday morning, and aided in suppressing the riot at Broome and Pitt Streets; subsequently, with Captain WILSON's command, patrol duty was done by them in infested portions of First and Second Avenues. In the afternoon they were part of Inspector LEONARD's command at the City Hall, and were engaged in punishing the mob which assailed the military at Broadway and Chambers Street. During the night they were among those dispersing the rioters threatening the Western Hotel, in Cortlandt Street; Wednesday, at the City Hall until the afternoon, when the force reported to Captain WARLOW, First Precinct; sent to Pier 4, North River, to quell disturbances there, and at night on duty in Broad and Stone Streets, where parties of thieves were attempting to break into stores. On Thursday dispersed mob at South and Wall Streets, threatening to break into a store and seize a negro employed there. The force remained at the First Precinct until Saturday A. M., when ordered to its own precinct on usual duty.

In this precinct a few officers in citizens' dress were constantly patrolling the ward, and mixing with the rioters in the colored district of Thompson and Sullivan, and marking the ringleaders. The block bounded by Sullivan, Grand, Thompson, and Broome is almost entirely occupied by negroes. The colored men were armed and prepared for a vigorous defence. They carried cart loads of stones to the houses, tore down their chimneys, and were well provided with missiles.

During the week Sergeant MILLER was constantly in charge of the station-house. He had special scouts out, and was thus informed of an intended destruction of the " Arch," in Sullivan Street. A prompt tele-graph by him of the fact to headquarters brought a force down in time to prevent it. He also received and took charge, during the first four days, of 268 refugees. During the week 751 were fed and cared for.

The record of the doings of this precinct is one full of honor, and the numbers injured and disabled in the first two encounters show how persistently and bravely they acted in order to accomplish a duty, even though it were an impossibility. The highest praise is awarded by Captain De Camp to Sergeant Ellison, who exhibited " dauntless cour-age," and to Sergeants Wade and O'Connor, as it is to all his men, of whom he speaks with a just and earnest pride.

Ninth Precinct.

Jacob L. Sebring, Captain, No. 94 Charles Street. On Monday, at 10 A. M., Sergeant Mangin, with ten men, reported to Captain Speight, No. 1190 Broadway, and were parties to the defence of the Provost Marshal's office there. At 11 A. M. Sergeant Smith, with a platoon, was also ordered to report to Captain Porter. Both of these officers and their commands were subsequently ordered to Forty-sixth Street, where Sergeant Ellison and force were so badly handled, a detailed account of which is given in the record of the Eighth Precinct. They arrived at the scene same time as Sergeant Wade, and went gallantly into the fight against overwhelming odds ; the list of casualties—Ser-geants Mangin and Smith and ten of the force being badly injured—shows how well and bravely they performed their part on this disastrous occasion. After the retreat they returned to their own precinct, escaping thither as best they could, and instantly reformed for further duty. At 5.30 P. M. the entire force, under Captain Sebring, reported at head-quarters. They were with Inspector Carpenter in the evening, at the exemplary punishment of the mob in the City Hall Park and Printing-house Square, and thence with him in the useful tour through the Fourth and adjacent wards.

At 1 o'clock A. M., on Tuesday, with the command under Sergeant Copeland, they went to Clarkson Street, to recover the body of the colored man hung, and which was cut down and taken to headquarters. At noon Captain Sebring, with his command, dispersed a gang at Spring and Murray Streets, who had sacked a liquor store and nearly murdered its proprietor. In the afternoon they were with Captain Dilks, in the visit to the factory in Second Avenue, and participated gallantly in the battle there.   In the evening they took a tour through the Fourth and wards adjoining.

Wednesday morning the Captain and command, with Sergeant COPE-LAND's force, visited the infected portions of the Second and Third Avenues, dispersing all crowds.   In the evening a section assisted the detectives in arresting gangs of thieves in Crosby and Houston Streets. At night the entire command were ordered to the Eighth Precinct to protect the " Arch," in Sullivan Street, populated by colored people. They charged the mob, beat and dispersed them, and prevented great destruction of lives and of property.

On Thursday morning the force was on miscellaneous duty, aiding as escorts to the military, guarding the prisoners at headquarters, &c. On Friday, same duties, which continued until noon Saturday, when ordered to their own precinct, and ordinary routine.

Sergeant SMITH was so badly injured at Forty-sixth Street as to be confined to his bed.   Sergeant SIEBERT had throughout remained in charge of the station-house, and proved equal to any emergency.   Col. LADUE, resident of the precinct, had formed a citizens' corps of " specials," and did patrol duty as well as acting for the protection of the station; and to him and the firemen of the precinct, who were of great service to Captain SEBRING, much credit is due.

During the entire week there was not a word of complaint from either officers or men.   Constant as was the duty, all orders were responded to with alacrity, and each one performed thoroughly.

Tenth Precinct.

Captain T. C. DAVIS, Essex Market.   At noon the reserve of this precinct was sent to Forty-sixth Street and Third Avenue, under Sergeants MINOR and DAVENPORT, and participated in the savage fight, heretofore described, which occurred there.   At 5 P. M. Captain DAVIS reported, with his entire force, at headquarters ; and in the evening, under Inspector CARPENTER, this force effectively used their locusts upon the mob which had attempted to burn the *Tribune* Buildings; thence in the risky march through the Fourth and other wards, and thence to headquarters for the night.   On Tuesday morning Captain DAVIS and his force, with the force under Inspector CARPENTER, went on the hazardous march to Second Avenue, and were prominent in the assault of the houses from which the police were fired at.   In this, four of the men of the precinct were badly injured, but all evinced a courage and determination which no danger baffled or checked.   Subsequently at headquarters, from whence they were ordered to the Fifth Regiment Armory, to procure the arms there and bring them to the Central Office for distribution; the men were desirous for more active duty and anxious to "flesh" their locusts again, but performed the duty promptly and well. At night Captain DAVIS and command were with Inspector LEONARD at the City Hall, where, on duty in various sections thereabouts of the city, they remained until Wednesday morning; then sent to Twenty-seventh Precinct station-house, sweeping away a threatening crowd in front of it; thence to the bonded warehouse in West Street, and thence to Twenty-seventh Precinct station again, where they remained on guard till late in the evening, when ordered to headquarters, and from thence to their own precinct.

On Tuesday officer JAMES ADAMS was accidentally shot in front of headquarters. He was conveyed home by a brother officer. This force did well and faithfully; and Captain DAVIS, his officers and men, won the honor that an entire and fearless discharge of duty entitled them to. Sergeant WEMYSS and Roundsman HART were especially active and valuable in all duties.

On the evening of Monday the station-house was attacked by a mob, who were driven off by officers WOOD and McCLOUD, and officer KING of the Third District Court, sundry citizens aiding, as did Surgeon WELLS and Sergeant GARLAND of the Seventh Precinct. Officer McCLOUD found a cannon in the building, and it was placed at the door, pointing on the mob; empty as it was, it had the desired effect—the rascals scattering.

On Monday an attack was made on the house No. 134 Division Street, and the furniture destroyed. Officer WOOD, of this precinct, and officer KING, of the Third District Court, with a number of citizens, made a charge on and dispersed the rioters.

At the attack on the lawless in Second Avenue, officer ROTHSCHILD was struck and badly hurt on the head, and officer SANDFORD also injured.

Eleventh Precinct.

JOHN J. MOUNT, Captain, Union Market. At six P. M. Monday, Captain MOUNT, with his whole force, reported at headquarters. At evening this command formed part of the force under Inspector CARPENTER, in the Park and Printing-house Square attack on the mob. The Tenth, being in the rear, had the last punishment of the flying, and put some fifty *hors du combat;* also, with the Inspector through the Fourth and other wards on same evening. On this tour Captain MOUNT and men were detached to protect the persons and property of colored people

near New Bowery and Roosevelt Street, the balance of the force continuing on their march.   The Eleventh did a hard duty well, kept the
mob in check, and ultimately drove them off.   Were rejoined by the
force, and detailed to the Fourth Precinct for the night.   At 10½ P. M.
repaired to Roosevelt and Batavia Streets, charged upon and had a sharp
fight with a mob of rioters and thieves, who were sacking houses, and
put them, with not a few badly injured, to flight.   The force were here
assailed from the roofs, and officer McMahon was very badly injured
by a brick.   A large bonfire had been made by the mob, of the articles
taken from the houses which were too cumbrous to steal—for the first,
last, and only purpose of the riots by every man and woman engaged in
them was theft, from a penny dip up to all things portable—and threatened to fire the adjacent buildings.   Captain Mount secured a length of
hose, and, attaching it to a hydrant, put the flames out—all the time his
force being the recipients of volleys of bricks and stones.   This done,
another fight was had with the rioters, who, for a while, boldly stood
their ground, but gave way finally, severely punished.

Tuesday morning the force were at headquarters, and, with Inspector
Carpenter's command, went to the Second Avenue.   On the terrible
assault the force received from the windows and roofs of the houses in
the vicinity of Thirty-fourth Street, Captain Mount, by order of the Inspector, led the storming party ; and gallantly did he do so, as the details
of this affair, already given, show.   One huge rioter was, on this occasion,
knocked clear off his feet and off the roof of a four-story tenement house,
by a single well-directed and well-dealt blow of a club.   He was
crushed to death by the fall.   Subsequently the force reported to Inspector Leonard, at City Hall, and were engaged several times during
the afternoon in dispersing the crowds in the Park and Printing-house
Square.   At midnight were at Western Hotel, Courtlandt Street, and on
guard there till 3½ P. M. ; back to City Hall ; there till 11 A. M. Wednesday ; and thence to headquarters, where orders to return to own precinct were received.   Here, with special force, patrol duty was performed until 6 A. M., when ordinary duty was resumed.

All officers and men of this precinct did their entire duty ; there was
not an exception ; and while each is entitled to the credit therefor, yet
especial mention should be made of Sergeants Polly, Ahearn, and
Reed ; Roundsmen Warmsley and Donohue ; Patrolmen Warren,
Beatty, Gass, Bogart, McMahon, and McCarty, for unflinching courage
and devotion to duty.   During the riots Sergeant Upham was left in
charge of the station-house and precinct, discharging his responsible duties there in a manner which restored confidence in the neighborhood,
and was most creditable to himself.

Sergeant POLLY was the officer who, with Inspector LEONARD, boldly entered into the midst of the mob assailing the military at Broadway and Chambers Street. They arrested the ringleader in order to divert attention from the military and draw it on themselves. The *ruse* succeeded and they were instantly assailed. They hung on to the prisoner, arrested another leader, and backed their way toward the City Hall, fighting at every step, and keeping the mob from them with their clubs. Inspector LEONARD is warm in his praise of the Sergeant's coolness and unflinching courage on this occasion—against the hundreds—and, indeed, no braver man is on the force. Both prisoners were held by these bold men, and the howling mob kept at bay until, as has heretofore been stated, relief from the City Hall arrived, when their assailants were attacked and beaten, and their prisoners cast off.

In connection with the Eleventh Precinct, it may be said that the German residents of that ward cannot have too much praise awarded them. They rallied to the aid of the authorities, and were prepared to assist them zealously, efficiently, and willingly whenever their services might be required. Another valuable force was also in readiness; at the Neptune Iron Works, Messrs. BOARDMAN & WATTS had organized three hundred good men and true for the protection of the ward. Two hundred were armed with sabres, one hundred with muskets, and all ready at a moment's notice to respond to any call. Woe would have fallen upon the rioters had they ever met them.

Twelfth Precinct.

Capt. A. S. RELAY, Harlem, One Hundred and Twenty-sixth Street, near Third Avenue. Early orders were received at this precinct, on Monday morning, to call in reserve and hold the force in readiness, but owing to the subsequent destruction of the telegraph, it was not until 5.30 P. M. that, by a special messenger, directions were received upon which Sergts. OSBORN and WALTERS left for headquarters with thirty-five men. They took the Third Avenue cars as far as Seventy-first Street, where, the operations of the road being stopped below, the company had concluded to haul off. The force thence took up the long march to headquarters, reaching there at 8 P. M. In the night they were with Inspector LEONARD's command at City Hall, and engaged on the various and constant duties required in that vicinity; portions of the time being the only force in Printing-house Square, and effectually keeping it clear of the ill-disposed. On Tuesday morning reported at headquarters, and, attached to Capt. WALLING's command, made the tour through the Bowery and adjacent streets; in the afternoon another tour to the Bowery and vicinity, under Inspector CARPENTER. On the return, one PATRICK CARLE stood on the sidewalk brandishing a sword, and threatening destruction to all in, and some out of, authority. Officer BANFIELD seized him, secured the weapon, and drew him into the ranks, conveying him to headquarters, where he was locked up. In the evening the command were at the City Hall again, and participated in the various excursions therefrom. On Wednesday morning the force were ordered to the Twenty-seventh Precinct, and thence to their own precinct, Harlem. They reached Harlem in the afternoon, and were received with enthusiasm by the residents. Although this force were not engaged on any very hazardous duty, yet they were actively employed, and what duties were assigned them were fully performed.

The few of this precinct who remained with Capt. RELAY and Sergeant SANDFORD, at the station-house, had very constant duty; they staid at request of citizens, who reinforced them with special patrolmen. The station-house was threatened on several occasions, but no attack made. At 3½ A. M., Tuesday morning, the premises at One Hundred and Twenty-ninth Street and Third Avenue were fired, and the force aided the firemen in their duties. About this time officer BERTHOLF, who was scouting, was attacked in the vicinity by six or eight men, and badly beaten; he continued, however, on duty. During Tuesday night three attempts were made to burn the Baptist Church on Fifth Avenue and One Hundred and Twenty-fifth Street, but were frustrated by the vigilance of the officers and specials; an attempt to fire the dwelling of EDGAR KETCHUM, Esq., on One Hundred and Twenty-seventh Street, was also prevented ; Sergt. WARES, discovering the attempt, gave timely alarm. There were no further matters of note in the precinct, except the visit, on Wednesday morning, of a gang of thieves, who, meeting citizens, would demand and take money from them. They were speedily driven away. The first arrest of this character of villains was made in Harlem by a number of firemen—Messrs. PETER GALLAGHER, THOS. GREEN, LUKE HOPE, and A. LISCOMB, of Engine Company No. 35, and CHARLES RIKER, of Hook and Ladder Company No. 7. These gentlemen, while on patrol, came across a gang of fifteen or twenty of them, and made an attack forthwith. A severe fight ensued, but resulted in the capture of four and the flight of the rest of the thieves. They were taken by their captors to the station-house, subsequently committed, and have been indicted. Of the courage of these gentlemen the police and citizens of Harlem speak in just terms of praise. So do the latter of the Captain and the force left there, whose well-arranged plans and constant vigilance were of the greatest value.

Thirteenth Precinct.

Capt. THOMAS STEERS, No. 178 Delancey Street. At noon the Captain, with Sergeants BIRD and SMITH, and twenty-five men, were ordered to Forty-sixth Street and Third Avenue, to report to Capt. PORTER. It was with much difficulty that they made their way as far as Thirty-fifth Street and Third Avenue, and here found it impossible to proceed further, the mob being overwhelming and threatening. The force, therefore, reported at the Twenty-first Precinct, East Thirty-first Street. Here great excitement prevailed, the mob gathering around the station-house, threatening to destroy it. Sergeant SAMUEL FORSHAY was in command, at whose request Capt. STEERS took charge and made arrangements to defend it, which deterred the rioters from further demonstrations. From this station Capt. STEERS sent conveyances for the wounded in the fight up the avenue and at Forty-sixth Street, and several were thus brought in. In the evening reported at headquarters, and were joined by the balance of the command, except Sergt. WOODWARD, left in charge of the station. The force were on picket duty around headquarters, and subsequently with Inspector CARPENTER in the attack on the mob in the Park, where they did considerable execution; thence, under same command, through the Fourth and other wards; over night at headquarters, and on Tuesday morning, with others, under Capt. SEBRING, gave the mob at Spring and Crosby Streets a severe defeat; on the same day were with Capt. HELME's command in the attack on the mob at Second Avenue and Twenty-second Street, where this force evinced great bravery, being among the first on the mob and into the building, encountering about fifty of the rioters armed with carbines, who, after a severe fight, were disarmed and terribly punished. The Thirteenth were subsequently engaged in the laborious work of securing and carrying down stairs the large number of carbines and loading them into the wagon which had been secured. After this work was done, and the entire command reformed by Capt. HELME, they were hemmed in from all directions by mobs, and would have had a bloody battle but for the timely arrival of Inspector DILKS and his command.

After the taking of the building, Capt. STEERS sent Sergt. LAFLIN, officers SEYMOUR and OSBORN, to seize a wagon for the purpose of loading it with the arms. They took one, emptied out its load, and, with the driver, brought it to the building, where it was used for the required purpose.

At night this precinct formed a portion of the force under Inspector CARPENTER in the attack upon the rioters at BROOKS BROTHERS' clothing store, Catharine Street, after which, from headquarters, it was ordered to the care of its own precinct, where the rioters had sacked Provost Marshal DUFFY's quarters in Grand Street, were robbing stores, and beating negroes. A short time before their arrival, a mob, led by a man since arrested and indicted, had been met at Pitt and Delancey Streets, and fired into by the military, and a number killed; the body of one of them was brought to the station about the time the force reached there. This had had a good effect, and deterred the mob from an attack on the station-house, threatened several times during the day, but each time boldly met and prevented by Sergt. WOODWARD, in charge. The force arrived at midnight, and at once were engaged in dispersing all gatherings in the precinct, saving and affording refuge to colored people, and, with a force of specials aiding, broke upon and scattered a mob about to destroy the "Hook," in Jackson Street. At every turn the rioters were subsequently met, no opportunity afforded them of uniting, and by Wednesday noon order reigned in the precinct. Then the force devoted themselves to recovering stolen goods, and during the week secured a large quantity. On Saturday resumed usual duty. All of this precinct did faithfully, finely, and it is just to make signal mention of *special* policemen BRAISTEED, WELSH, BARRETT, and TOOKER, whose efficiency and courage were especially noticeable.

Fourteenth Precinct.

Capt. J. J. WILLIAMSON, No. 53 Spring Street. The force, under the Captain, Sergeant MACKEY accompanying, on Monday reported in full at headquarters at 4 P. M., being among the earliest, and accompanied Inspector CARPENTER to Broadway and Amity Street, where such a bold and successful fight was had with a mob, and where the locusts of the Fourteenth were active in strewing the ground. At night were at the City Hall, under Inspector LEONARD, where a full share of the responsible duties in that section was performed by them.

On Tuesday were sent, Sergeant ULMAN in command, with Capt. PETTY's command, to disperse the rioters at the soap factory in Sixteenth Street; and afterward, under Capt. HELME, were engaged in the recovery of the arms at Twenty-second Street and Second Avenue, where the terrible fight was had, and where, but for the steady courage of the men, they would have been overcome. In this affair the Fourteenth, under Sergeant HUGHES, were closely engaged, and many of them had narrow escapes; they acted together and made havoc among their opponents, some of whom they pursued far beyond where safety would suggest. At night they were at BROOKS BROTHERS' store, under Inspector CARPENTER, where again their steady courage was evinced. It was a sharp, quick, hard fight, and well won. The night was pitchy dark. The command came on to the mob gathered at Catharine, Hamilton, Cherry, and Oak Streets. A platoon charged into each street. The Fourteenth took Oak; had hand-to-hand fight, but cleared it of everything living. In the melee officer REGAN became separated from his force, and was chased into a hallway, from which he escaped to the rear, and fled over fences and sheds. He received bad injuries in jumping to the ground, but saved his life. After this affair a march was made through the Fourth Ward, and several collisions with the rioters had,—in all cases the latter being speedily dispersed; thence the command marched to the Fifth Ward; at West Broadway and Leonard Street they were unexpectedly attacked with shot and stones; made a rush, swept the rioters right and left, and cleared the vicinity. Soon after returned to headquarters, where they were held in reserve until Friday, then returning to routine duty at their own precinct. On Wednesday morning twenty-five were sent to Yorkville, under Roundsman STEERS, where they were of the greatest service.

At 11 A. M. Wednesday, officers SUTTON, RILEY, DUBUAR, and CANNON, of this force, were detailed to pilot a regiment to JACKSON's foundery, Twenty-eighth Street, between First and Second Avenues, which had been threatened. At Twenty-third Street and First Avenue the military were fired on by the mob; the attack was continued through Twenty-third to Second Avenue, and on the Avenue to Twenty-fifth Street, without any response; here, however, the howitzer was unlimbered, and the mob fled. The line of march was resumed, when the mob rallied and renewed the assault, continuing it till the foundery, on Twenty-eighth Street, was reached. Soon after the military reached it they were again assailed by the mob which had followed them, and by another from the First Avenue. There was a delay in getting into the building, the doors being locked, and the mobs were firing and pressing down. The military thereupon fired several well-directed volleys, killing and wounding a number, and causing a dispersion. Until late next day the foundery was constantly besieged and threatened by large mobs, but the determination of the military kept them at bay.

The fury of the rioters appeared to be directed against the four policemen; a committee waited on the officer in command and demanded that they should be delivered up; if not, the foundery would be stormed at all hazards; he was assured if they were delivered up the mob would disperse. The committee stood at a respectful distance while delivering their message, and took to their heels, on an intimation to do so or they would be shot. At 1 P. M. Thursday, the four of the Fourteenth, disguised in old garments of workmen which had been found in the foundery, made their way out, mingled with and through the mob, and succeeded, unmolested, in reaching headquarters.

On all the duties this force were engaged in they were up to the requirements, on no occasion failing to respond faithfully and gallantly.

Fifteenth Precinct.

Capt. C. W. CAFFRY, No. 221 Mercer Street. At 9 A. M. Monday, Sergeant McCREDIE and fourteen men reported to Capt. SPEIGHT, at No. 1190 Broadway, and were sent to Third Avenue and Forty-sixth Street. Reaching the avenue from Forty-third Street, a crowd was found extending to Forty-sixth Street—a mass of excited, belligerent people. Here the small force of the Fifteenth was joined by more of the police, making in all forty-four. The mob met them defiantly. Sergt. McCREDIE— Fighting Mac, as he is familiarly called—took command. The regulars, beaten by the rioters, were fleeing down the avenue pursued by the mob. The Sergeant ordered a charge, which was instantly and gallantly made ; the mob was driven back to Forty-sixth Street, prostrate men marking the advance of the force; at Forty-sixth Street, where they expected to meet more police, none were to be seen; the mob rallied and soon poured down the avenue again, and crowded it in the rear from the side streets ; they numbered thousands; they made an overwhelming charge from above upon the force; stones, bricks, &c., from street and houses, from front and rear, filled the air ; clubs, iron bars, guns and pistols were used upon them; the men attempted to keep together, but it was in vain ; the force broke before the mass and fled, each for himself; those who took the side streets were the most fortunate; those who ran down the avenue were not only pursued and beaten by the mob which had charged on them, but had to run the fearful gauntlet of the one below. Of the fourteen men of this precinct engaged here, nine were injured—several seriously. All those who escaped reported as soon as possible to the station-house.

In this battle and retreat officer BENNETT was knocked down three times before he ceased fighting; the last time he was senseless. He was robbed of every article on him save his drawers, beaten savagely as he lay in the street, and left for dead. After the mob passed on he was conveyed by some strangers to St. Luke's Hospital. Here he was thought dead, and placed in the dead-house by order of some one in charge, where he remained several hours. His distracted wife, ascertaining where he was, hastened to him. She could not believe him dead; discovered that his heart pulsated; flew to the officials and begged their aid. He was removed into the hospital buildings, restoratives applied, and he revived, but remained unconscious for three days. His condition for some time was critical.

Officer TRAVIS, at the defeat and separation of the force, started down the avenue; his foremost pursuer had a pistol; he wheeled, knocked him down, and secured the weapon; before he could use it others were on and upon him; he fell beneath a score of clubs, was stamped, jumped upon, and otherwise terribly assailed; his jaw was broken, his teeth knocked out, his head terribly cut, his right hand broken, and he left for dead, after being stripped of every article of clothing, even to shirt and stockings. He was subsequently carried to St. Luke's Hospital.

The retreat down the avenue was under a shower of shot and stones. Officer PHILLIPS also ran the gauntlet, receiving many head and body blows, and, on turning into Thirty-ninth Street, made for the open door of a residence, but it was closed against him. At this moment one of his pursuers, in soldier's clothes, fired a musket, but,· missing him, clubbed the weapon, and assailed him. The blow was caught, and the musket wrenched away. PHILLIPS, almost blind with blood, and staggering from exhaustion, clubbed the fellow down, and another run for life was had, during which the musket was thrown over a fence; he made across lots in rear of Third Avenue, to Fortieth Street, but here was headed off by a portion of the mob; a woman rushed upon him, and making a blow at his neck with a shoemaker's knife, missed her mark and split his ear; another lunge, and it made a severe wound in his arm. At this juncture some one, evidently of influence in that section, came to his rescue and threatened with death any one who made further attack; he took PHILLIPS' club, and by his determined manner succeeded in keeping them off and getting him to the Thirty-first Precinct station. When the mob met him at Fortieth Street, a little fellow of some thirteen years sought to save him by running up, grasping his hand, and claiming that he was his father, beseeching them not to kill him. His entreaties were of no avail, and, but for the interference of the party mentioned, his fate would have been a hard one.

Sergt. McCREDIE, on the charge, was struck on the wrist with a bar of iron and badly injured. On the retreat he was attacked by four men, and knocked down two; he fled into the house of a German family, and was instantly secreted by a young woman there between two mattresses; the mob soon came rushing in; searched the house from cellar to garret without success; were told that the Sergeant had ran through and escaped by the rear way, and left satisfied it was so.

Officer SUTHERLAND was knocked down with a brick, then beaten till insensible—from head to foot a mass of gashes and bruises. He was picked up when the mob left him, and conveyed to St. Luke's Hospital. Officer

MINGAY was badly beaten on head and body. The crowd only left him when they thought he was punished enough. Officer TERENCE KIERNAN, after receiving a stunning blow on the back of the head with a stone, a blow on the back of the neck with a hay-bale rung, and a blow on each knee about the same moment, fell; while prostrate and nearly insensible, the wife of Mr. EAGAN, who saved Superintendent KENNEDY, threw herself on his body and cried: "For God's sake, men, do not kill him." This restrained the mob, and they passed on; he, KIERNAN, was carried into a house, minus his coat, vest, cap, and shield; the shield was afterwards given to him by Mrs. EAGAN, who picked it up, covered with blood, in the street. He was subsequently disguised and smuggled out. In coming down, he called at the Croton Cottage, was recognized, but, by a clever dodge, escaped. Not so with the cottage; in less than an hour afterward it was in flames.

Officer BROUGHTON, on the charge, was cut in head and face, one of his eyes almost destroyed, but went twice into the fight after being injured. Officer GABRIEL received enough body blows to make a jelly of him, but none that proved serious.

While Sergt. McCREADIE'S section was thought safe at Forty-sixth Street and Third Avenue, the off-platoon, under Roundsman THACHER, consisting of eighteen men, was sent to reinforce him. They reached the scene after the defeat, without knowing of it, and were instantly and desperately attacked. A bold fight was, for a time, made, and a running retreat, in tolerably good order, ensued. The fight throughout was hand to hand, the men injured receiving club blows. Officer BODINE'S head and face was a mass of wounds, and his clothes were stripped from off him. He was rescued and brought to the station in a wagon. Officer FOSTER was cut on the face and head, badly bruised on the body, and, in running the gauntlet of clubs and stones on the avenue, was knocked down fourteen times; he fainted after escaping his pursuers, and was taken by citizens to the station. All of those who were able to, reported promptly at the precinct.

Officers DIDWAY and GIBBS of this platoon arrived too late at the station to join it, and so followed it up. On reaching Forty-sixth Street and Third Avenue, and knowing nothing of the defeat of their comrades, they turned into the avenue, and were forthwith set upon by the mob; they fought their way back as best they could. Officer DIDWAY, after receiving much injury, and a terrific blow on the head, which forced his eye out of the socket, managed to find safety in an alley-way, from whence he was taken to his home. Officer GIBBS fought as long as he could see, fell beneath the blows, and was then kicked, beaten, stoned, and left for dead. He was conveyed to St. Luke's Hospital by some residents of the vicinity so soon as the mob left him. Of the injured in these two fights, officers BENNETT, TRAVIS, and GIBBS were long unable to do duty.

In the afternoon a portion of the force were with Inspector CARPENTER in the defeat of the mob at Broadway and Amity; here one of the ringleaders was captured by Sergeant ROE, and another by officer BAR-HEBT; both were severely punished, and were lodged in the station near by. Fourteen knapsacks filled with plunder were dropped on the street by the rioters, and taken charge of by the police. At midnight the force returned to its own precinct.

On Tuesday morning to Central Office; subsequently, with Captain HELME's command, to Second Avenue and Twenty-second Street. In the severe fight here, this command were unflinching and valuable; Sergeant BLAKELOCK was fired at, the ball grazing his cheek. Returning to the Central Office, were ordered to report to Inspector LEONARD, at City Hall, and were engaged on guard and other duties thereabouts. At night were with Inspector CARPENTER's command in the attack on mob at BROOKS BROTHERS' clothing store, and on the subsequent tour and skir-mishes. Returned to Central Office, and thence to own precinct for the night. Captain CAFFRY received word that Broadway was infested with highwaymen; Roundsman THACHER, with six men, started on patrol, and at one o'clock arrested three highwaymen, two of whom have since been sent for ten years to State Prison; they had met, knocked down, and robbed a Mr. SEARLES, in front of the Jones House. Next morning the force returned to the City Hall, where they remained, engaged in divers duties, until Saturday, when ordered to their precinct on usual ser-vice.

The Fifteenth have won great credit for the amount of services ren-dered and the courage and fidelity with which they were performed. The number of wounded in the various engagements was fifteen, of which eleven were very seriously injured—a greater list of casualties, probably, than in any other precinct. On all occasions they were willing and effective. Sergeant BLAKELOCK was sick in bed when he heard of the riot, but at once reported himself for duty; he served bravely through the week, and then went to bed again more ill than before. Sergeants DILKS, McCREDIE, and ROE, with Roundsmen THACHER and LEFFERTS, are entitled, with the men, to all commendation, and the Captain bestows it lavishly.

While on guard duty in Park, Tuesday evening, officer HECTOR MOORE came across two men garroting a returned soldier; he arrested both of them, and they have since been sentenced, by Recorder HOFFMAN, to fifteen years each. Six others arrested by the officers of this precinct are awaiting trial for highway robbery, and two for riot. At the fight at Leonard Street and West Broadway, Sergeant ROE was fired at, the ball cutting off the tip of a finger.   Sergeant DILKS was invaluable to his command during Riot Week, as he was to other commands to which he was attached.   On all occasions he was cool and courageous.   The first intimation received by the Captain of the very serious character of the riot was when his men came in, on retreat, bringing some of the wounded with them.   Six doctors were at once engaged in attending to the latter. On the retreat of McCREDIE's section from Forty-sixth Street, men and women from adjoining houses, for want of other articles, hurled household furniture and crockery at them.

Sixteenth Precinct.

Captain H. HEDDEN, No. 156 West Twentieth Street.   At 5 P. M. Monday the force was at Central Office ; at night at City Hall, under Inspector LEONARD, where employed till morning.   On Tuesday morning Captain HEDDEN and force were part of Inspector DILKS' command in the battle at the factory, Twenty-second Street and Second Avenue, where the officers and men had severe encounters ; the rioters, at close quarters, clubbed their muskets, and fought desperately ; but it was of no avail ; down they went and over were they run. At this time Sergeant WRIGHT was disabled by a blow with the but of a musket, as was also officer WARNER, in hand-to-hand encounters.   Many others of the force were injured, but not seriously.

At the above battle one of the parties of rioters attacking the Sixteenth were under the lead of a man who exhibited great courage ; his comrades were driven back and he retreated under terrific and deadly punishment; turning to escape, and even then dying, as he reached the sidewalk he tripped on the curb and staggered head foremost on to an iron picket-fence ; one of the pickets entered under his chin, penetrating to and into the roof of his mouth.   Thus horribly impaled, his head suspended, his body stretching to the ground, he died,—there being, by friend or foe, no opportunity at the time of extricating him.   The attention of Captain HEDDEN was subsequently attracted to his shocking position, the body was taken down, and laid on the sidewalk.   It was found, to the surprise of all, to be that of a young man of delicate features, white, fair skin.   Although dressed as a laborer, in dirty overalls and filthy shirt, underneath these were fine cassimere pants, handsome rich vest, and fine linen shirt.   He was evidently a man, in intelligence and position, far above those with whom he had been in fellowship.   It was impossible at the time to take possession of the body, as further attacks by the rioters were constantly expected.   Nothing of the identity of the

party is known; the body, left with those of the others killed, found a
grave with them.   This is a suggestive incident, and, were it possible to
have secured the remains, a revelation of great importance as to the in-
stigators of the riots, it is thought, would have been made.

At this same fight a rioter came rushing out of the factory having a
carbine with sword-bayonet attached.   He made a desperate assault upon
one of the officers of the Sixteenth, the bayonet cutting through the coat-
sleeve and just missing the arm; withdrawing it and about to make
another and more successful thrust, he was felled to the earth by
members of this command, and died soon after.   The carbine was
so firmly clutched that it was with great difficulty taken from his grasp.
He was accompanied from the building by a lad who clung to his coat.
One of the officers caught him up, carried him out of harm's way, and he
ran shrieking off to a bevy of women who had been urging on the
rioters.

Tuesday evening the Sixteenth repaired to the City Hall, and were
sent, under Captain HEDDEN, to Thomas Street, near West Broadway,
where, coming upon a mob destroying the dwellings of colored people,
they made a charge and scattered it.   Before daylight, Wednesday, were
on duty protecting Western Hotel, Courtlandt Street; the mob here fled
to Greenwich Street, and, re-collecting, attempted to break in and rob a
shoe store there; this precinct followed and beat them off; in the course
of the melee pistols were used by the mob, but without effect.   This force
also repaired to the U. S. Bonded Warehouse, Greenwich Street, which
was being attacked; on nearing it they received a volley of shots from
the rioters, but made a bold charge, and, after a brisk fight, drove
them off.   The mob had broken into the building and were about setting
fire to it when Captain HEDDEN and his command assailed them.

On Wednesday evening Sergeant WRIGHT and ten men were detailed
to the United States Marshal's office, where they remained till Saturday.
The balance of the force, on Wednesday, did escort duty at the funeral
of Brig.-Gen. WEED, and afterward were sent to Hudson and North
Moore Streets, where a crowd threatening a mission school was punished
and driven off; thence a march was taken through the Fifth Precinct,
and all gatherings dispersed; in the evening they visited Pier No. 4,
North River, and prevented a renewal of the outrages there.   This closed
the active duty of the Sixteenth; it remained in reserve at the Hall until
Saturday morning, when ordered to its own quarters.

The Sixteenth, officers and men, emulated each other in effectively
doing all they had to do, and found no risks too great to encounter, no
duties too arduous to perform.

Seventeenth Precinct.

Capt. S. Brower, First Avenue, corner of Fifth Street. Early on Monday morning the Captain, with his force, reported to Capt. Porter, at Forty-sixth Street and Third Avenue. When reaching there the crowd was not large, but soon the rioters assembled in force, coming in fifties and hundreds from different sections, until swelled to thousands of excited men armed with clubs and other weapons. The first overt act was the stoppage of the Third Avenue cars, the taking off of the driver and horses, and compelling the passengers to get out. The force attempted to prevent this, but were driven back. Then ensued an attack on the Marshal's office, a shower of stones breaking doors and windows, and finally the mob rushed into the building, beating back the small force who valiantly opposed them, until flight or death were the alternatives. The force retreated into Forty-sixth Street, where they were engaged in saving the occupants of the building and their property—the premises having been fired—until they were again beaten back by overwhelming numbers. Sergeant Finch arrived about this time and took command, Capt. Brower going to the station-house. The Sergeant made, with his force, a charge upon the mob, but failed to disperse them, and received a severe gash from a blow on the forehead, which subsequently laid him up, and his force was compelled to retreat. The mob was a huge one, thousands composing it, and the opposing force, bravely as they did, were entirely inadequate. After the discomfiture here, they reported to headquarters, and in the evening, under Capt. Brower, were at the Park with Inspector Carpenter, where they made havoc upon the mob in the grand charge heretofore detailed; thence through Fourth Ward and to Central Office for the night. On Tuesday this precinct joined Capt. Petty's command in the visit to the soap factory in Sixteenth Street, and aided in restoring order in that section. They were also with Capt. Helme's hazardous expedition in the Second Avenue, and took a liberal hand in the severe fight there; they were among those storming the building in which the stolen guns were stored, taking it after a savage fight, and recovering a large number of arms. At night Sergt. Slote and ten men were detailed for duty to Gen. Wool, remaining until quiet was restored. At midnight Capt. Brower took command of one hundred and fifty men, marching through the Eleventh, Thirteenth, and Seventeenth Precincts, returning to headquarters Wednesday morning. At 9 A. M., in command of his own and the Eighteenth and Nineteenth Precinct forces, he proceeded to the scene of riot and murder in Thirty-second Street, between Sixth and Seventh

Avenues, dispersing the crowd and recovering the body of the colored man hung there, bringing it to headquarters.

This was the last of the active duties. In the Forty-sixth Street battle Sergeant FINCH was severely injured; Sergeant SLOTE was, subsequently, the only officer acting with Capt. BROWER, Sergeant GRIFFITH being deputed to the telegraph office, and Sergeant WEITH left in charge of the station-house. The conduct of every man was, throughout, of the most creditable character, and the Captain alleges that he wants to lead no better men in any emergency, never mind how great.

At the fight on Forty-sixth Street, the force were, of course, powerless. Officer HILL was badly hurt; officer WEILL was so badly injured as long to be unable to resume duty; and some four or five others were wounded. On this occasion women were active in urging on the rioters. The fight was hand to hand, and the force did bravely against overpowering numbers.

When the force was in Second Avenue fight under Capt. HELME, after the charge upon and capture of the building where the stolen arms were secreted, officer TYLER secured a gun; he coolly went into the street, and procuring from a soldier, whom he found in the vicinity, several rounds of ammunition, loaded his piece, and then started, alone, down Twenty-second Street toward First Avenue, where the mob had retreated, firing upon them until his ammunition was exhausted. He was all this while made a target of from the mob and from houses on the street, but escaped unharmed. Officer TYLER had been under fire at Bull Run, and brought the experience of "shot and shell" home with him. His bravery was the subject of laudation among the officers and men of his precinct.

Eighteenth Precinct.

Capt. JOHN CAMERON, No. 163 East Twenty-second Street. This precinct is in the heart of the lately infected district, and the station-house was destroyed by the mob. On Monday the Captain had great trouble in calling in his men, because of the many who had individual interests to look after in the care of their families and property, both, from their connection, being threatened. Early in the morning Sergt. VOSBURGH, with a section of men, was sent to the riot at Forty-sixth Street and Third Avenue. Here, with the overpowering mob, they had a severe fight, in which officer WYNNE was severely beaten about the head and stabbed in the arm—was hurt the worst of any of the force, and was conveyed to the hospital; officer LARUE, so injured as to be laid up for several days; officer SANDERSON beaten, and his clothes nearly all torn off, and others more or less injured. The force, when at-tacked, was on its way to join Capt. PORTER, but found it impossible to do so; after a brave struggle, they were compelled to retreat and scatter, making their way back to the station as best they could. In the after-noon a number of the force, under Sergeant BANFIELD, took charge of the Armory on Second Avenue, until relieved by the Broadway Squad.

At 5.30 P. M. Capt. CAMERON reported with force at Central Office, Sergeant BUCKMAN and three men being left at station. Remained at headquarters over night, and on Tuesday were engaged with the com-mand under Inspector DILKS, in the attack on the mob at the Second Avenue factory, and the storming of the building filled with armed rioters. Subsequently, the Captain, with his force, was on the expedi-tion to the soap factory in Sixteenth Street, which had been threatened, and then, with Capt. HELME's command, to Second Avenue and Twenty-second Street again, where such severe fighting and such perils, as al-ready described, occurred and were encountered. At night, held in re-serve at headquarters.

On Wednesday Sergeant VOSBURGH, with the force, formed part of Capt. BROWER's command, which visited Thirty-second Street, near Sixth Avenue, and recovered the body of the negro hung there. On the same day the force was divided—a portion ordered to report to Capt. SPEIGHT, Twenty-ninth Precinct, and a portion to Capt. HUTCHINGS, Yorkville. Capt. CAMERON remained at headquarters, where his services were active and valuable. On Wednesday night Officers McCORT and McVAY, of this precinct, did guide duty for the military on the march through First Avenue, and were in the disastrous conflict in which Col. JARDINE was so seriously injured and the military driven back.

On Thursday, what few of the force remained at headquarters as-sisted the detectives in arresting one of the ringleaders of the mobs—the notorious ANDREWS—in a colored rendezvous in East Eleventh Street. On Friday the force sent to Yorkville returned, as did those sent to Capt. SPEIGHT, and went on guard duty in the vicinity of headquarters. On Saturday the force were detailed to usual duty in their own precinct; their own quarters had been burned down, and they found temporary ones at the Central Office.

Sergeant BUCKMAN, with three men, were left in charge of the station-house on Monday. An immense mob, the accumulations from down-town and up along the East River, had passed and threatened it in the morning, but made no serious demonstrations against it that day. On Tuesday Sergeant BURDEN relieved Sergeant BUCKMAN, and about 4½ o'clock P. M. received a visit from the mob; with his men he barricaded the windows and doors as best he could, and then they made their escape

5

through the prison in the rear, having to pry off the iron bars of a window, and into Twenty-third Street. The mob soon after broke in and set fire to the station; the bellringer on the adjacent tower struck the alarm once, but was threatened with instant death if he did not cease and abdicate; both of which he very sensibly consented to do.

When the Broadway Squad were attacked, and likely to be overwhelmed in the gun factory, Sergeant BUCKMAN, in citizen's dress, made his way to the building, and, by direction of Capt. CAMERON, advised their retreat from it, which was successfully made. After the fight with the Broadway Squad at this armory—and the record, when reached, will show how bravely this squad behaved—Capt. CAMERON sent a number of his men, in police uniform, with sedan chairs, to take charge of the killed and wounded of the rioters. The mob allowed the police to enter into their very midst, offered them, on their errand of mercy, no molestation, and three of the misguided victims were taken by them to Bellevue Hospital. The Captain placed his faith for the safety of his men on the "sedans," and he was right. In this fight some seven or eight of the rioters, who, on the mob gaining entrance, had rushed up stairs, were burned to death, their comrades having fired the building from below.

On returning from the hospital, to which he had been aiding in carrying one of the rioters, officer GRUBELSTEIN was set upon and chased by a mob in Twenty-fourth Street; he jumped over divers fences, and reached Twenty-third Street—here again met, he ran for Third Avenue, thence to Twenty-first street, and into a lager-bier saloon, where he was for a while secreted; came out and was again recognized and given chase to; managed to evade his pursuers and jump into a cellar, where he remained until dark, when he made his way to his home. He was much hurt by the pelting from stones, sprained his ankle in getting over the fences, and was laid up for several days. This was his return for carrying the wounded of the mob to the hospital.

Since early Monday morning it was unsafe for a policeman to show himself. While on post Monday, before riot had developed, officer ARNOUX was attacked by a gang; he managed to escape to the station minus hat, club, and portions of his clothing. The officers and men of this precinct lost, in the destruction of the station-house, from $3,000 to $4,000 in bedding, clothing, and other personal property. Not an article was saved.

The record of the Eighteenth shows hard and constant duty and much personal loss and injury. They were in critical positions frequently, but were always equal to them, and throughout contributed largely to the honorable repute which the entire force has made for itself.

Nineteenth Precinct.

Capt. G. T. Porter, East Fifty-ninth Street, near Third Avenue. The riots commenced in this precinct, an excited crowd collecting, about 9 o'clock A. M., at the Provost Marshal's office, corner of Forty-sixth Street and Third Avenue. This was soon swelled by arrivals from all directions, until thousands had assembled, many of them armed with clubs and other weapons, and all demonstrative of mischief. Capt. Porter repaired to the office, stationing a portion of his force—in all sixty men—in front, and the balance inside of the building. The drafting commenced at 10¼ A. M., and was uninterrupted for some twenty minutes. Meantime the mob outside, increased to huge proportions, were feeding their excitement with threats and execrations, and suddenly turned their attention to the Third Avenue cars, one of which was passing down. The cry "Stop the cars!" was raised, a rush was made, the drivers taken off, horses detached, and the passengers compelled to abdicate, two of them relieved of their watches; a section of the police went to the rescue, and were assailed with clubs and stones, overpowered and driven back. Having committed the first overt act the mob became frenzied, and at once made a rush on to the Marshal's office, assailing the force on the street, driving them into the building, and showering into the windows stones and all kinds of missiles. To fight or to keep at bay the thousands was an impossibility. The Marshal and his clerks, with the police, were driven back with clubs through the building, and escaped from the rear. In a few moments the furniture was destroyed, piled up and fired, and the building was in flames so speedily that two families living up stairs barely escaped with their lives. The police repaired to the adjoining buildings and attempted to save the property in them. They were fiercely attacked and driven away. The firemen reached the scene, but were prevented from doing anything. The Chief Engineer was present, and addressed the mob, urging them to allow the firemen to go to work. Meantime the fire had spread rapidly, and three of a row of brick buildings were in flames; the mob yielded to Chief Decker's appeal, the companies went to work, and the fourth house was saved. It was about this time that the rioters made the first serious demonstrations against the police. Hitherto, in the progress to arson and pillage, they had driven them away, but had not concentrated against them; now they massed on the Third Avenue, and made a furious attack on the force with pistols, clubs, and stones. Very soon officer Cook was knocked down and seriously injured, and several others badly hurt. The aid sent to Capt. Porter from below could not reach him, and were themselves engaged with another portion of the mob ; resistance against the overwhelming numbers was madness, and, after a brief but gallant fight, the force broke and fled, the mob masters of the situation. The men recollected at the station-house, and, in citizens' dress, revisited the section where they were defeated, and succeeded in bringing off those of the injured who had remained there. In the evening the entire force were ordered to headquarters, and with Sergeant COPELAND's command visited Clarkson Street, for the recovery of the body of a colored man murdered there.

Tuesday, a portion of the Nineteenth, under Sergts. BUMSTEAD and HOLMES, were, with Inspector DILKS' command, on its expedition to Second Avenue and Twenty-second Street, and were engaged in the severe and obstinate fight there. Subsequently, under Sergts. BUMSTEAD and FULMER, a portion revisited that vicinity with Capt. HELME's command, and were again participants in another severe engagement, and were of the storming party which carried the building filled with rioters. About daylight on Wednesday, Capt. PORTER took his command, and made a tour through the Thirteenth and Seventeenth Wards, and later they were with force sent to recover the body of the colored man murdered at Seventh Avenue and Thirty-second Street. About noon, Sergt. BUMSTEAD, with squad, made an onslaught upon a gang at Bleecker and Thompson, who were bent on destruction of dwellings thereabouts. A brisk charge and liberal use of the locusts sent them in all directions.

On Thursday the force was returned to its own precinct, where Sergeant DECKER had, with two or three men, been left in command.

The Nineteenth was the force first attacked by the rioters, and they were in all the principal engagements. The officers and men exhibited an alacrity in responding to calls upon them, and a steady courage throughout which rendered them reliable and valuable.

Twentieth Precinct.

Capt. G. W. WALLING, No. 352 West Thirty-fifth Street. Early Monday the reserve of the Twentieth were sent to the Seventh Avenue Arsenal, where it remained till noon, and in the afternoon Capt. WALLING, with Sergeants ROONEY and CAREY, reported at headquarters with force. In the evening made an expedition to the Eighth Ward, which was found quiet, and thence reported to Inspector LEONARD, at the City Hall. Were engaged in the scouting expeditions sent out by the Inspector, and in the guard duty done in the vicinity of the Hall. Tuesday morning were returned to Central Office. From here made an expedition to Pitt Street, but too late to have a hand in punishing the mob, the military, a short time before, having met, fired upon and killed a number of them.   On return to headquarters this force were sent to the upper part of the city, in the vicinity of the Twentieth Ward, where the mobs were reported as having it all their own way.   ALLERTON's Hotel, Eleventh Avenue, between Fortieth and Forty-first Street, had been sacked and burned; a body of military had been beaten, many of the soldiers wounded, and a number of their guns taken away.   Hearing that the Sixth Avenue Railroad stables were being attacked, Capt. WALLING hurried with his force to them.   The report proved untrue, but he received information that the rioters were in Forty-seventh Street, near Fifth Avenue, attacking the fine private residences there.   Thither the force went on the double quick, coming with a rush upon the mob, a portion of which had just forced an entrance into the basement of Dr. WARD's residence, while other portions were at work on other dwellings. The rioters ran on the first charge.   The force broke into squads of threes and fours, giving vigorous chase; every man with a club or other weapon who was overtaken was clubbed to the sidewalk, and laid there. The streets were speckled with the carcasses of such.   Many dropped their weapons, but did not escape the penalty for carrying them.   The route was complete; the punishment inflicted severe.   The sole purpose of this mob was robbery.   They were interrupted just as the spoils were thought secure.   Up to this period they had undisputed sway, had been doing an immense amount of damage, and kept that entire section of the city in a state of terror.   The force reunited at Forty-seventh Street and Fifth Avenue.   It was here ascertained that when Capt. PUTNAM's regulars were in that vicinity, one of them, who was sick, had fallen behind and been set upon by the mob; he was knocked down, beaten, kicked, and then thrown senseless over a fence into a lot on the Fifth Avenue. Capt. WALLING and his force hunted him up, and he was conveyed to Bellevue Hospital.   The force returned to the Twentieth Precinct Station-house, where, matters looking threateningly on Ninth Avenue, dispatches for military aid were sent by Capt. WALLING.   The mob had cut down the telegraph poles on Ninth Avenue from Thirty-seventh to Forty-third Street, and had used the wire in fastening wagons and carts together, making barricades of them across the avenue at Thirty-seventh and Forty-third Streets, and at the junctions of the intervening streets. At 6 P. M. Capt. WESSON's regulars arrived at the station-house.   Capt. SLOTT (of the Twenty-second Precinct) took command of a body of the police, and, with the military in the rear, marched to the avenue and Thirty-seventh Street.   Here the force made an attempt to remove the barricades, but were met with a discharge of firearms and stones from the rioters beyond. They had to fall back; the military advanced to the right and fired several volleys; the mob retreated, and the police, again advancing, removed the barricade. Soon after they were again rallied on by the mob, and the military again took the right, loading and firing as they advanced, the mob falling back, finally fleeing, and the police removing each barricade as it was reached. This work done and the force returned to the station-house, where it was held in reserve. At 9 P. M. an attack was made upon a gun and hardware store in Thirty-seventh Street, between Eighth and Ninth Avenues; Sergt. PETTY, with a force, was soon there, and soon had the thieves flying, save three who were left senseless on the sidewalk. At midnight a mob attacked the colored church in Thirtieth Street, between Seventh and Eighth Avenues. Capt. WALLING, with his entire force, came upon them while busily engaged with axes in the work of destruction; they had concluded not to burn the church lest some premises thereabout occupied by their friends would be injured; so the axe was brought into requisition, and right actively being used. The force charged upon the mob unexpectedly, but were met with a discharge of guns and pistols from the street, alleys, and doorways. The fire was returned, and the clubs resorted to; scores of heads were cracked, many of the lawless were stretched at length, and in a few moments there was not an "upright" rioter to be seen.

This was the last of the more active duties of the Twentieth; they continued at the station-house doing scouting duty, and making some expeditions until Saturday, then resuming regular patrol. The services of this force were of the greatest value; they were in a badly infected vicinity, had hazardous and arduous duty to perform, and have made for themselves, by their faithful and brave discharge of it, an honorable name in and out of the department.

Sergeant PETTY was left in charge of the station, and, just as the force on Monday evening was leaving for headquarters, Superintendent DAVIS, of the Colored Orphan Asylum, led into the station two hundred and sixteen of the children, none over twelve years of age, who had escaped from their home by the rear as the dastardly and infamous mob forced an entrance in front and fired the building. These little ones would undoubtedly have been assailed had they not been hurriedly guided away. They were sadly terrified on reaching the station, but were reassured, housed and kindly cared for by Sergeant PETTY until sent to the Island.

When the force were returning to the station from the severe usage of the thieves at Forty-seventh Street and Fifth Avenue, sundry women on Fifth Avenue, on Thirty-fifth Street, and on Sixth Avenue, assailed them as "bloody murderers," &c., &c.

On Wednesday evening some women visited the station, stating that they had soldiers secreted in their houses, who had thus escaped the fury of the mob on Tuesday, when the military were defeated in the vicinity of ALLERTON's Hotel. Capt. WALLING sent a coach, with an officer in citizen's dress, and collected three, returning them to the Arsenal. The coach, while on Fortieth Street, was attacked by the mob, the windows and doors broken in with stones, but, with a courageous driver and good horses, got off without further damage.

When the force hurried to Forty-seventh Street and Fifth Avenue, on the mob about to sack residences there, they met crowds of women and children with bags and baskets, waiting on Sixth Avenue, above Forty-sixth Street, for the word to join in and gather the plunder. After the fight these women were busy attending the wounded.

On Thursday morning at 2 o'clock, a party of four or five of the force discovered a gang which had broken into a pawnbroker's shop in Thirty-ninth Street, near Eighth Avenue, and were rifling it; they had secured a number of guns and sabres, when this small force made a dash upon them, beat them badly, and recovered all the property.

On Tuesday afternoon, Capt. WALLING, while alone and reconnoitering at Thirty-fifth Street and Eighth Avenue, saw three men staving in the door of Mr. HEISER's hardware store, Eighth Avenue, above Thirty-fifth Street. He ran up and grappled one of them, and, dealing a powerful blow with his club, knocked him down; an officer came to his aid, and disarmed another, who, with his companion, escaped. The fellow knocked down was got on to his feet by some friends, and helped, staggering along, to Thirty-sixth Street, where he fell senseless; he was bundled into a wagon and carted off. When the Captain made this attack, a mob was awaiting, at the corner of Thirty-sixth Street, the success of their comrades' attempt to break open the store, when they would have rushed to its pillage.

Sergeant PETTY several times, during the absence of the force, was threatened with destruction of the station-house, but made excellent preparations for a sturdy defence, by barricading, &c. At one time he had over four hundred refugees under his charge, and all were made comfortable, and given an abundance to eat.

Twenty-first Precinct.

Capt. A. M. PALMER, No. 120 East Thirty-fifth Street. The Captain, with his command, was in the battle with the mob on the morning of Monday, at the Provost Marshal's office, Forty-sixth street and Third Avenue. All the forces engaged, it will be recollected, were repulsed.

On the return to the station, the Captain went home, and, in consequence of the stoppage of the Third Avenue cars, could not get back again until Tuesday morning, when he reported with his command to the Central Office. The force was with Capt. PETTY's command on that morning at the disturbance in the vicinity of Sixteenth Street and Tenth Avenue, and the balance of the day and night on general duty at the Central Office. On Wednesday morning they were returned to their own precinct, and in the afternoon the Captain, being sick, went home, and Sergeant BRACKETT took command. The force were kept in reserve in the precinct, portions being constantly on valuable scouting and picket duty. All that night and all Thursday were gangs around, armed with clubs and other weapons, threatening dwellings, howling, hooting, and terrifying citizens; the stores were all closed and terror reigned. Sergeant BRACKETT's well-arranged plans of operating in detail, boldly seconded by his men, prevented any concentration or more serious demonstration during this period. At 7 P. M. Thursday, officer CHANDLER was brought to the station badly beaten, and was thence conveyed to the Bellevue Hospital. He had been attacked at Thirty-fourth Street and Second Avenue by a gang, against which he made manful fight, but uselessly. During the night the Sergeant and his force continued on the *qui vive*, and no outrages occurred. They were in squads, here, there, everywhere, and, although in an infected district, by their promptness, activity and intelligent movements, frustrated attempts at outrage.

On Friday morning Sergeant BRACKETT in command, with Sergeant HASTINGS and thirty-five men, repaired to Thirty-ninth Street and Second Avenue; the Seventh Regiment was their escort; the block between Thirty-ninth and Fortieth Streets, and the First and Second Avenues, were surrounded by the military. This was a thoroughly riotous district, and the police went to work entering every house and searching it for goods stolen during the riots, from the cellar to and on the roof. Not a room, a closet, a cubby-hole, or a "between beds" was missed: every nook, corner and hole was investigated; sometimes the inmates were searched with success; the explorations were continued in similar manner to Thirty-third Street, each block being surrounded by the military. At 4 P. M. the military were unfortunately withdrawn and the search had to cease. But an immense amount of property had been recovered, among it a full wagon load of fire-arms, bayonets, pikes, &c., in all 173 pieces; furniture, groceries, dry goods, &c., &c., comprised the rest. Among contraband articles taken were five steel-headed clubs, villainous and murderous weapons, which the owners had prepared for their work of murder and robbery. On Friday search by squads was renewed and another large amount recovered, among it some $400 worth of the property of the slaughtered Col. O'BRIEN, found at a house in E. Thirty-fourth Street, where the thieves secreted it.   This active work was kept up for several days, and with constant success.   Sergeant VAUGHAN with fourteen men, and Roundsman MOORE with six, each in different portions of the precinct, recovered thousands of dollars' worth.   The catalogue of the goods re-taken by the Twenty-first would make a large volume.

Although this force had but one encounter with the mob, their services in their precinct were invaluable.   They prevented many serious demon-strations, and in the duty of recovering goods were zealous and unflinching, notwithstanding its hazardous and unpleasant character.   They have saved many thousands of dollars, by their efficient discharge of this duty, to the treasury.

Sergeant BRACKETT, on whom the command devolved, is entitled to great credit for the sagacity characterizing his action throughout, while his associate officers and the men have won a full share of the honors on the record.

Twenty-second Precinct.

Capt. J. C. SLOTT, Forty-seventh Street, between Eighth and Ninth Avenues.   On Monday morning Sergeant WILLIAM M. GROSS and twelve men reported to Capt. PORTER, at the Marshal's Office, Forty-sixth Street and Third Avenue.   Here was the first serious demonstra-tion of the mob, and the first attack upon the police, in which the latter were defeated by overwhelming numbers ; this force returned soon after noon to the station.   Capt. SLOTT, with Sergeants ALDIS, POTTER, and MURPHY, and the command, reported at headquarters in the evening, from whence they accompanied Inspector CARPENTER and force to the Park ; participated in the charge upon the Printing-house Square mob, and contributed to the strewing of the ground with the bodies of the lawless and riotous.   Thence were on the tour through the Fourth Ward, at the fight in Roosevelt Street, and the subsequent skirmishes.   At midnight were at headquarters again, but soon after sent to the Twen-tieth Precinct Station to protect it and its hundreds of refugees.   They remained here until Thursday, when ordered to their own precinct.   Meantime, however, they had participated with the Twentieth in the ac-tive, vigorous fight with the mob which, at midnight Tuesday, were at-tempting to destroy the colored church in Thirtieth Street, between Seventh and Eighth Avenues.   They went into this under "shot and shell," but every man with a will and determination that largely aided in the speedy and, to the rioters, costly victory.   This command was also in the storming of the barricades in Ninth Avenue; from Thirty-seventh to Forty-third Street. Capt. SLOTT, of the Twenty-second, was in command of the police here, and, after a charge made under a shower of bricks and shot, only withdrew his men long enough to let the military discharge a volley, when the force pressed forward again, took and removed them. So, nearly all the way up, on approaching each barricade, were they under fire from street or house-tops, but made a clean sweep of all the obstructions. Several of the rioters were killed in this engagement. The force returned to the Twentieth Station. In the afternoon of Wednesday, Capt. SLOTT made an expedition to Forty-second Street and Tenth Avenue, clearing the coast there; subsequently, Sergt. ALDIS was sent with command to Twenty-seventh Street and Seventh Avenue, where rioters were rampant, did the work of dispersal thoroughly; on returning, when near the arsenal, was ordered by Gen. SANDFORD to take his force and a company of military, then awaiting him, to Forty-second Street and Tenth Avenue, where the mob had again gathered, and were threatening to burn the residence of Mr. CAMPBELL. He at once wheeled, and with the added force of military, hurried up. The force was, on arrival, greeted with shouts of defiance, and with shots and missiles from doors, windows, and house-tops, as well as from the street. He halted, and tried a little moral suasion, begged of the rioters to desist and to retire; they gave him no heed, and the officer in command of the military made a similar appeal. The only responses, save from a few who got out of the way, were renewed yells and volleys. The military then wheeled into sections on the avenue, one facing up the other down, the police in the center, and opened fire. Men were shot down in the street, some picked off from the house-tops, and others from the windows, where they had been actively firing. In a few moments the mob was entirely dispersed, leaving their dead lying in the streets uncared for. This ended the "battle-field" operation of the Twenty-second, who were relieved from the Twentieth Precinct on Thursday, retiring to their own on ordinary duty. Capt. WALLING, of the Twentieth, speaks in eulogistic terms of the valuable services of this command while at his precinct, and the history of their arduous and responsible duties, so well performed, more than justify him. Every call was promptly, cheerfully, and bravely met, and more honor won by them for an organization which is now laden with honors.

Twenty-third Precinct.

Capt. HENRY HUTCHINGS, East Eighty-sixth Street, near Fifth Avenue. The force of this precinct were, on Monday, left without orders, in consequence of the cutting of telegraph wires, until about 6 P. M., when a special messenger brought orders to report at the Central Office. Promptly starting, they were in time to be with Inspector CARPENTER's command on its visit to the mob in the Park and Printing-house Square, and to join in the compliments so liberally bestowed upon the heads of the fleeing rascals. The force were on duty with the Inspector until returned to headquarters at midnight, and soon after were ordered, under Sergt. COPELAND, to the recovery of the body of the negro hung in Clarkson Street. This duty was performed in a rain drenching every man to the skin, and, as they were returning to headquarters, the command received the information that Mr. WAKEMAN's house, on Eighty-seventh Street, opposite their station, had been sacked and fired, that the station-house had also been consumed, and every article belonging to the force stolen or burned. Doorman EBLING, who was left in charge, managed to save the telegraph instrument, but that was all. This entailed heavy loss upon officers and men.

Before they had breakfasted on Tuesday, this force were with Inspector CARPENTER on the expedition in Second Avenue. At Thirty-fifth Street an assault was made on the rear, and simultaneously, with guns and missiles, from the tops and windows of a block of tenement houses on the avenue. Here the charge was ordered by Inspector CARPENTER upon the houses, and during it fierce hand-to-hand fighting ensued. A portion of the Twenty-third were among the assaulting party—the balance being busily engaged with the mob on the street. On this occasion a large number of the rioters were so punished as never to be able again to participate in similar scenes; they fought desperately when finding themselves cornered in the houses, and the orders were " no prisoners." In the afternoon a portion of the force, under Sergeant HICKS, was ordered to Broadway, by Commissioner ACTON, to employ or press into service for the Commissioners thirty-two stages. The force secured fourteen, being all they could find running. During the night the men were repeatedly called in readiness for duty, but were not required. On Wednesday morning it was thought necessary for the force to return to Yorkville to their own precinct, which they did, reaching it by steamboat at 1 P.M. On landing, arriving at Fourth Avenue and Eighty-sixth Street, they were greeted by the citizens enthusiastically. The mob had, for two days and nights, been rioting there, unrestrained; universal alarm prevailed, and neither lives nor property were safe. Where the excesses would end no one could tell, and this opportune arrival of those who would and could protect them caused the greatest relief and a general joy. All was quiet in the precinct after their arrival; active patrol and scouting duty were performed during the balance of the week. A portion of the force was at once engaged in making search for stolen property, and succeeded in recovering a large amount—among it most of Mr. WAKEMAN's valuable library. A number of the rioters and thieves were also arrested, while the search was being prosecuted.

During the absence of the force the rioters had sacked and burned Mr. WAKEMAN's residence, had sacked and burned Mr. GREY's, and had sacked the dwelling of Provost-Marshal NUGENT; the station-house had been burned, as had the large grocery store of Messrs. METTER & DEM-AREST, which was pillaged of a very large amount of goods ere it was given to the flames. The rioters and thieves had no opposition offered them for the first forty-eight hours, and much money had been obtained from citizens, on whom they called and demanded certain amounts under threat of destruction of their persons or their property. All this the presence of the force promptly put an end to.

While acting from headquarters, the Twenty-third were prompt, active, gallant, and their efficiency was felt in all the services in which they were engaged. In what repute they are held at home is evidenced by the cordial reception on their return, and by the immediate fleeing of the villains whom their absence had encouraged to acts of outrage and plunder.

Twenty-fourth Precinct.

Captain JAMES TODD, Steamboat No. 1. The force of this precinct constitute the Harbor Police. On the morning of Monday Captain TODD, on hearing of the riot, volunteered his command for service in any way useful. The first order received was about noon, from Major-Gen. WOOL, to collect all the military at Governor's Island, and bring them to the city, which was promptly obeyed, and the troops landed at North Moore Street at $2\frac{1}{2}$ P. M. In the afternoon special duties were performed between the city and the island; arms and ammunition were brought over for the Custom House, Sub-Treasury, and other Government buildings; others were furnished by this force for the defence of the ram *Dunderberg*, lying near WEBB's ship-yard, and which had been threatened with destruction; muskets were also brought for the defence of the buildings threatened at Printing-house Square. Patrolman BLACKWELL performed a hazardous duty in the conveyance of the arms from the landing to their destination, but did it with a sagacity which prevented suspicion, and prevented in every case interference. At midnight, by request of Col. O'BRIEN, this force went to Governor's Island, procured arms and ammunition, and conveyed them to four hundred men of his command then at Staten Island Ferry; thus at 4 A. M., armed and equipped, they were enabled to be in the city.

Tuesday the force started to Riker's Island to bring down five hundred of the military from that place; carried an artillery company to Governor's Island, where it was provided with guns and ammunition, and thence to the city. The balance of the day and until Wednesday morning, constantly and rapidly steaming from point to point on the river, keeping watchful eyes on all quarters. On Wednesday morning large bodies of police and soldiers were carried to Yorkville and to Harlem; in the afternoon Captain WILSON and his force were conveyed to Washington Heights. At all these places the appearance of "Police Boat No. 1," with its freight, was joyously hailed. At 10.30 P. M., while patrolling the river, the fire at the Atlantic Dock Elevators was discovered. Capt. TODD at once ran his boat to the spot, and commenced throwing water from the engine on board upon it; it was of no use; the force fought the fire until they were driven off by the heat, their own safety endangered; then attention was turned to saving other property; three Government prizes loaded with cotton were in proximity to the flames; the force speedily grappled them and towed them into the bay, where they were anchored. Returning to the scene of the fire, again were in service there attempting to extinguish it, until daylight, when off to Riker's Island, from whence more troops were brought to the city. Thursday was occupied, by order of General SANDFORD, in bringing troops from the islands, conveying some four hundred colored refugees—the orphans among them—to Blackwell's Island; carrying arms and ammunition to Harlem for a volunteer corps there, and patrolling the river. On this day this force were parties to the rescue of the colored man beaten and thrown overboard at Pier No. 4, North River; the man was taken on board the police boat and brought ashore. On Friday a large number of "contrabands" were taken to Blackwell's Island, and active patrol duty performed. When Captain TODD took his first and largest cargo of contrabands on board, the excitement against them being high, he adopted every expedient to keep them out of sight. They were stowed on the boat in most admirable style, and not a "woolly head" would have been recognized as on board. How he did it; how he compressed so much flesh and blood in the limited space at his disposal, was as much a matter of curiosity to him as to others.

While the Twenty-fourth was not in any of the conflicts of the week, the services of the force were active, arduous, and wearisome; they were, too, of the utmost value, especially in the rapid pouring of troops into the city, and in the prompt supplies of arms and ammunition. The saving of the Government prizes at the Atlantic Docks was important service. Captain TODD and his men have established the great value of this arm of the service, and the public acknowledge their obligations for services so willingly, faithfully performed, and so preservative of its safety.

Twenty-fifth Precinct.

Captain MILLS, No. 300 Mulberry Street. The force of this precinct is popularly known as the " Broadway Squad." The Captain was absent on leave during the Riot Week, and the command devolved on Sergeant BURDICK. At noon the Sergeant, Roundsmen FERRIS and SHERWOOD, with thirty-two men, reported to Captain CAMERON, of the Eighteenth, and were ordered to the care of the gun factory at Twenty-first Street and Second Avenue, with orders to hold it at all hazards until aid arrived. The men reached the establishment by going singly or in pairs, thus escaping the serious attention of the mob, which was rapidly gathering around it—concentrating from all quarters, in gangs from the tens and twenties to the hundreds. But thirty-five officers and men were in the building. A request was made by the Sergeant, of those in charge, to stop work and close up the factory, but was declined because of the absence of the proprietors and consequent want of orders. Very soon the mob made demonstrations by word and act, but were warned off by Sergeant BURDICK, who notified them that any one making an assault would do so at his peril. The mob left, retiring up the avenue, but after an absence of some fifteen minutes, returned reinforced to thrice the original number, and instantly surrounded the building, yelling like demons ; they were armed with all kinds of weapons. The force determined to hold the building, and an attempt to fire it was defeated ; each of the squad was armed with a carbine, furnished by the factory, and was judiciously stationed. But now stones began to be hurled through the many and low windows; the mob, constantly increasing and encouraged, made an assault ; entrance was demanded and refused ; the squad kept cool and determined ; but a sledge-hammer in the hands of a brawny rioter was at work on the door; the lower panel was broken in ; a shout of exultation from those around, and down on his knees he went and crawled partially through ; an instant and well-directed shot from one of the force strewed his brains in all directions, and he was hastily dragged back by his friends, dead. This sudden catastrophe to their leader staggered the mob, but only temporarily, for in a few moments the attack was renewed with the greatest violence ; the windows were showered through with stones, and shot came thick and fast. Sergeant BURDICK sent to Captain CAMERON, and called for the aid expected ; the Captain sent word that it was impossible for his force to reach them, and that the expected aid had not arrived ; soon orders were received to save his men and retreat from the building. By this time the thousands were pressing on to success ; the " Broadway Squad," by a determined front, had, for four hours, held them in check, but to do so longer was impossible, and to remain was certain death; the order was given to retreat. There was but one way in which to do so and escape the infuriated crowd; neither to the front or the sides was it possible; and the only way of safe exit was through a smoke hole in the rear wall, about twelve by eighteen inches, and some eighteen feet from the ground; this led into the yards from Twenty-first Street.   Not a moment was to be lost. Boxes were piled up to reach the spot, and the men, one at a time, squeezed in and through, feet foremost, performing rapid gymnastic feats outside in swinging to and dropping from a gutter-trough to the yard below.   Thus the entire force made their escape, and the last man was only out when the mob were in, and the work of pillage and arson commenced.   From the yard into which the men had dropped they had to climb over into a stone yard, and through that go on a keen run to the Eighteenth Precinct Station in Twenty-second St., reaching it unharmed. Here their stay was short; the mob, enraged at the obstinate holding of the factory, had got scent of them, and would have made short work of the station and all in it.   So Sergeant BURDICK sent the force off singly or in squads of two and three; but about all had to seek shelter under kindly roofs, and doff their uniforms ere they could reach headquarters in safety.   But they all did reach the Central Office unharmed, and at 5½ P. M. were sent on picket duty in the vicinity, which was performed until Tuesday morning.   On Tuesday morning the force was with Inspector CARPENTER's command in the Second Avenue, and were parties to the severe fights there, having a serviceable hand in the exemplary punishment meted out to the rioters.   The "Squad" had the right of the line, and made the charge on the liquor store, at Thirty-first Street, from which the rioters were firing and hurling stones.   They forced the doors and were in and through it; in the course of the clearing process that ensued, one man, who was freely using his gun, and fought savagely, was knocked square out of the window, and was dead before he reached the ground.   Seven blows from the locusts were his portion.   In the afternoon they were again under Inspector CARPENTER in the tour through Third Street, First Avenue, and Houston Street.   At 5½ P. M., with Captain BOGART's command, the "Broadway Squad" proceeded to Twenty-ninth Street and Eighth Avenue, where a mob was sacking the residence of Mr. J. S. GIBBONS, No. 19 Lamartine Place.   The force came upon the rioters, made a bold, steady charge, and drove through them to the house, strewing the way with bodies as they went. A large number of rioters and thieves were inside of the building, and while a portion of the command went in, others remained at the front, to receive with the locusts the villains driven out.   It was here that the unfortunate DIPPLE, of the Twenty-fifth, received the wound which caused his death. A fellow came rushing from the house, laden with plunder, was caught by Sergeant BURDICK and knocked down; he had not released his hold of the thief ere a score of bullets whistled around his head, two of them lodging in the body of his prisoner, and six of the police fell at the discharge. It appeared that the military, who were stationed a short distance away from the house, on seeing the rush of the rioters from it, had fired recklessly and without orders, injuring more friends than foes. Officer DIPPLE was shot in the leg, the ball shattering the bone, and splitting, part passed into and up through the marrow; he was conveyed to the City Hospital, but the peculiar character of the injury induced inflammation of the brain, and he died on the following Sunday. Officer HODGSON was shot in the right arm, a ball and three buckshot passing through the fleshy portions. Officer ROBINSON received a severe flesh wound in his thigh.

The work being accomplished here, the force returned to headquarters, where they were held in reserve until Wednesday morning, when they reported to Captain HELME, Twenty-seventh Precinct, remaining with him until Thursday A. M.; returning to Central Office, they were ordered to patrol Broadway in force, from Canal to Twenty-fifth Street. In the evening dismissed, and next day on regular duty.

The "Broadway Squad" is composed of the tallest men in the force, none being under six feet, and most of them over. They afforded good targets, and how the heavier proportioned ones ever squeezed out of the gun factory, as described, is as much a mystery to them as it undoubtedly is to the reader. It shows what marvelous feats men can perform when under the propulsive influence created by the thousands of a murderous mob close on to their heels. The defence of the factory was nobly, though uselessly, attempted, and persistently made until orders from headquarters came to withdraw. The "squad" acted here, and on all occasions where true courage was necessary, as became brave men; and Sergeant BURDICK speaks with just pride of a command of which any man might be proud. Popular as the "Broadway Squad" has always been, its efficiency during "Riot Week" has enhanced its reputation.

The military, at the defence of GIBBONS' house, made a charge after their unfortunate volley, and the man whom Sergeant BURDICK was holding had two bayonets run through and through him. Officer MORRIS, of the Twenty-fifth, was the first to enter GIBBONS', and, meeting a rioter, broke his club at the first blow, but knocked senseless his man. Roundsmen BENSON SHERWOOD and JEROME H. FERRIS are entitled to mention as having been most courageous and valuable. They were the associate officers of Sergeant BURDICK, and their courageous and intelligent services were largely instrumental in winning for the force the proud name it has acquired, neither of them understand the word "flinch," and they were ever first in duty and in danger. Both are brave, chivalrous men.

Captain N. R. MILLS was at Sangersfield Center, Oneida County. So soon as he heard of the riot he telegraphed to know its proportions, and whether he should return. After waiting for reply he took the first train and came directly through, reporting at Central Office for duty on Thursday evening, and took command of his force. He was off on sick leave.

On Monday officer WELLS, of this force, while on duty in the vicinity of the Astor House, heard the cry of "Nigger, nigger!" and hastening to Park Row, met a mob chasing a car and endeavoring to enter it. Single-handed he kept them back, and went in, finding a colored man, frightened nigh to death, and bleeding from a blow on the head. When the cars reached the terminus, opposite the Astor House, he took the man out; the mob closed on him, but he threatened death to the first who made an assault; getting to the Astor House steps, with the aid of citizens the man was concealed from the sight of his pursuers behind one of the pillars, and the poor fellow was subsequently taken home by some gentlemen present. A few minutes after, an Amity stage came down with a negro on the box; the mob caught sight of him, came back and attacked the omnibus and all inside and out with stone; the driver was compelled to stop, and put the negro off. Officer WELLS went to his aid as the rioters were about to seize him; the mob threatened murder to both; a citizen came to the rescue, drew a revolver, and, with officer WELLS, kept the cowards at bay. They were followed by the mob down Barclay Street to Church, where, just as a rush and overthrow was about being made, a squad of the Third Precinct appeared, who rattled the skulls of the ruffians and sent them flying in all directions.

Twenty-sixth Precinct.

Capt. THOMAS W. THORNE, City Hall. Early on Monday thousands of excited people were gathered in the Park and Printing-house Square. Incendiary harangues were made, and threats uttered; every colored man met in the vicinity was attacked and beaten. Capt. THORNE detailed five of his force, in citizens' dress, who mingled with the different crowds, and reported every fifteen minutes. At 5½ o'clock P. M. the force with Capt. WARLOW's command reported to headquarters, and were sent thence to the First Precinct, through which tour was made. On returning at dusk, met by citizens at the Post-office, who informed them of attack on *Tribune* Building. Started up Nassau Street at double-quick, came

6

on the crowd of five or six thousand, the work of destruction having been commenced, the office entered, gutted, and fired.   Capt. THORNE gave the word to his men to keep together.   The order to charge was given, and on they went, without waiting to estimate odds, the handful, with a ringing cheer, against the thousands ; the first blow was received by the Captain, a bludgeon on the head, knocking him back six feet ; down went the man who gave it by the locust of officer COWEN ; on went the men, dealing blows right and left, desperately and with fearful effect ; the mob, even with its proportions, could not stand the impetuous charge ; they fought a few moments, surged back, and then again swung forward, as though to crush out the force; it was too late; on and among them were the command, nearly every blow bringing to the ground a rioter ; in one place, six lay so close as almost to touch each other; it was too much for the lawless, and, after hard and hand-to-hand fighting to Frankfort Street, they broke, fleeing in wild confusion.   That portion which went up Chatham and Center Streets were closely followed for a while, and severely clubbed by this force ; that portion which fled across the Park were met by Inspector CARPENTER and his men, and scores knocked down.   No mercy was shown, and over a hundred lay in the square and Park, the well-punished victims of their own folly and crime.   While the mob were being thus terribly handled in the street, some of the force turned their attention to the *Tribune* Building, fighting their way to and entering it. The fire had but just been lighted, and was readily extinguished.   Officer McWATERS, on entering the door, was assaulted by a burly ruffian, armed with a hay-rung, who, by a powerful blow on the shoulder, knocked him down ; instantly on his feet again, he more than repaid on the heads of the rioters the blow.   The building was cleared speedily, and not a man found in it escaped without severe punishment.

This good work being in detail so bravely and thoroughly accomplished, Capt. THORNE ordered his force to cover Spruce Street and the square at Frankfort.   Sergeant DEVOURSNEY took command.   What of the crowd had returned from Chatham Street and Center were pushed back to Frankfort, and the space below entirely cleared.   Meantime rumors were constant of mobs accumulating up-town to come down and finish a work which had been so disastrously for the rioters foiled.   About eleven o'clock the mob had reassembled above Frankfort Street, though not in the old proportions, and were pressing sharply upon the police thrown across the square.   Sergeant DEVOURSNEY used every argument to induce them to retire, and these failing, ordered, " Now, men, go in and give it to them !" Go in they did forthwith, and, where moral suasion had failed, the locusts succeeded.   It was a quick, severe fight, and a number were so badly punished as to be unable to get away.   This was the last serious demonstration in that section, the determined action and success of the police furnishing a lesson which was laid to heart.

After the attack at the *Tribune* those laying in the street were allowed to be carried off by their friends returning for them, and the square looked somewhat like a field of battle. In the charge ordered by Capt. THORNE, very many of the locusts were broken by the men of this precinct; pretty good evidence that when they hit they meant to hurt. When the mob was being driven off, the writer of the "Record" came very near experiencing the locusts while attempting to reach the *Times* Building. But for the prompt recognition of officer FRANK BROWN, of the Twenty-sixth Precinct, who rushed forward and warded off three well-raised and well-aimed clubs, he would have had a serious and practical experience wherewith to speak of "locusts." Sergeant DEVOURSNEY was in the crowd alone and edging his way to the *Tribune* office just before the mob broke into it; he had got on to the sidewalk, and drawing his revolver was about to shoot the man cheering on the crowd, and who was also engaged in breaking in the door; several bold and good citizens were there, endeavoring to dissuade the rioters from their work, and they crowded around the Sergeant, one of them seizing his arm and begging him to desist, that he would do no good, would sacrifice his own life, besides exciting the crowd to a frenzy; heeding the wise advice he forced his way back, got to the station, found Capt. THORNE had been telegraphed to, hurried back, heard the cheer of the gallant force on its charge from Nassau, went in with his locust and fought his way through and to them, joining in the general fight. When it is remembered that the Sergeant was in uniform, his conduct exhibits the truest courage. Officer McCORD was in citizen's dress, and going to the assistance of his comrades was hit and hurt by mistake. Officer GARDNER received a serious blow from a brick on the leg. An elderly gentleman, who was among those at the *Tribune* office, attempting to dissuade the mob, was hurt on the head by the police, who, of course, were ignorant of his purpose in being there. He was taken to the station-house, had his wound dressed, and asked if it would leave a scar. On being told it would, he said he should wear it proudly. The wounded who were not carried off by their friends were conveyed to the Twenty-sixth Precinct station-house, where Police Surgeon KENNEDY, with two assistants and half-a-dozen attendants, were busily engaged in washing, bandaging, sewing and strapping. The room had all the appearance of an army hospital after a battle—the floor covered with blood, bandages, lint, surgical instruments, pails of bloody water, with Surgeon KENNEDY, his shirt-sleeves rolled up, examining, dressing, and ordering. His cool, systematic and quick appliances showed him to be master of the situation. There were wounds of all descriptions—the incised, contused, lascerated, punctured, and pistol-shot. All were cared for, and the Doctor's kindness of heart glistened through the cool exterior of the skillful surgeon.

On Tuesday morning this force, Sergeant DEVOURSNEY in command, with Sergeants VAN HAGAN, PELL and TOWNSEND, reported to Central Office, and, with Capt. WALLING's command, made tour through Tenth and Thirteenth Wards; Capt. WALLING's command were heartily cheered at several points on the march. Subsequently, with the force under Inspector DILKS, they were in the engagement at Second Avenue and Twenty-second Street, where Capt. HELME's command were met; here the Eighteenth Precinct was detached to visit their station-house on Twenty-second Street, near First Avenue, and the Twenty-sixth were ordered to accompany; many of the mob, which had been dispersed, had fled into the houses below, and the force marched down under a heavy fire from roofs, doors, and windows; when about half way they halted, but stood firm, and Inspector DILKS sent down the military to their support; taking the right, they at once commenced firing, clearing house-tops, windows, and doors, pouring in shot wherever a head was shown, and thus progressed down the street, clearing it also of a reassembled mob; thus was the march had to the station-house and to First Avenue. It was a severe ordeal for the police, who had no weapons with which they could retaliate. On the return from First Avenue, Sergeant DEVOURSNEY hung back, reconnoitering. He was fired at from a window, the bullet grazing his head. An officer of some other precinct, who had a musket, was with the Sergeant, and he deliberately loaded and discharged his piece, with careful aim, several times. The subsequent march with Inspector DILKS was had and risks incurred, all the men eager for the fray; but with the police there was no further collision, though they were, until below Twenty-first Street, pretty constantly under fire. Soon after reaching headquarters, this precinct, with Capt. BOGART's command, visited the Sixteenth Ward, thence to Mr. GIBBONS' house, No. 19 Lamartine Place, which they then found safe, and started on return. From here Sergeant DEVOURSNEY, with officer GARDNER, fell back to reconnoiter, and were stoned by different gangs; many women assured them that they " would all be killed like rats before they left the ward," and vituperation was constant. At Twenty-eighth Street and Eighth Avenue DEVOURSNEY was informed that a mob, on disappearance of the force, had again speedily collected at Mr. GIBBONS' house and were sacking it. Promptly notifying Capt. BOGART, the force were wheeled, and, some military accompanying, were, on the double-quick, speedily at the spot. The military were held in reserve, the force, part of it, rushed in the house, the balance kept in front and a portion to the rear; the caged plunderers,

men, women, and half-grown children, were all badly punished save the
last, who were spared; not one of the men escaped; those who rushed
out were all loaded with spoils, and were met by the police in waiting,
only to go to the ground.   One rioter made a rush from the door, pistol
in hand, and was caught and clubbed by officer HILL; the fellow fired,
the ball inflicting a serious wound in the officer's thigh.   At this time it
was that the military most unaccountably fired upon those in front of the
house, wounding six of the police—one since dead—and killing two rioters.   The man who had shot officer HILL was riddled with balls.   Officer
RICE was shot in the groin, and had two slugs through the thigh.   He had
been doing good battle.   A ball passed through the sleeve of Sergeant
PELL.   One great, burly ruffian, covered with blood, jumped down from
the parlor window.   Officer HANIFER met him, and a fierce, brief fight
ensued, in which the locust seemed to have no effect; he escaped to the
street, and there a multiplicity of them brought him to the ground.
One woman, of goodly size, rushed out loaded with stolen goods; she
made fight like a tigress, seized an officer by the throat and attempted
to strangle and bite him; it was necessary to punish her before she released her hold and spoils.   Many women who were in the house were
caught, and from a rather respectable looking one was recovered shawls
and other articles stowed around her person; one grim-visaged, brutal
looking fellow rushed out with a bundle of music as his plunder; despite
the good taste of the selection he marched to the music of the locusts.

This was a trying occasion for the police; at one time they were
under two fires, one from the military, and the other from the rioters in
the house.   The unfortunate DIPPLE, of the Broadway Squad, was the
only one who lost his life; officers RICE and HILL were long unfit for duty.
In the ordeal there was no quivering or flinching, fearful as it was.   At
the conclusion of this exciting affair an attempt was made to close up the
house, but as it had been sacked of everything portable, and the doors
and windows all smashed and useless, it was impossible to do so.   The
command returned to headquarters and were the recipients, from Commissioner ACTON, of a handsome and appreciative speech.   The Twenty-
sixth were held in reserve at Central Office until Wednesday morning,
when they were returned to the City Hall, and were in active service
until Friday, on the various scouting expeditions sent from thence by
order of Inspector LEONARD, and on the duties of guard and picket.   On
Friday returned to station and resumed usual duty.

It will be noticed that Capt. THORNE was not with his command on
Tuesday.   On the arrival of Inspector LEONARD, on Monday night, with
his large force at City Hall, he appointed Capt. THORNE his Aid, in the
many onerous and responsible duties which the protection of the

lower part of the City entailed. It was on Tuesday that constant vigilance had to be exercised to prevent the concentration of the crowds in and around the Park; from an early hour great excitement existed among the rabble gathering there, and, in checking it, the police experienced the utmost difficulty; but despite any and all they succeeded. During the morning the Inspector and his Aid had been responding to orders from headquarters, sending off detachments to different sections, and by no 'n they were stripped of the entire command, and were left with but one doorman. On the disappearance of the force the mob quickly concentrated, and made demonstrations against the station-house. Inspector LEONARD at once ordered it closed and secured, and, with Capt. THORNE, hurried to the Central Office, promptly returning with a sufficient force to again disperse the crowd, though not without some trouble and hard knocks. From this time until Friday, when Inspector LEONARD dismissed his command, Capt. THORNE was constantly under his orders, and executed them with an intelligence and promptitude which more than justified the sagacity of the Inspector in selecting him.

Of the conduct of the officers and men of this force, from the commencement of the disturbances down town to conclusion of the riots, but little need be said. The record shows what they did, and how officers and men emulated each other in fidelity to the public interests, and in the gallantry with which they defended them. Their duties were wearying and almost unceasing, yet performed at all times with cheerfulness and alacrity. The "Twenty-sixth" can carry with honest pride their designating number, and justly can Capt. THORNE say, as he does, " I am proud to sign myself their Captain."

Twenty-seventh Precinct.

Capt. JOHN C. HELME, No. 117 Cedar Street. On Monday afternoon the entire force, except Sergt. ROCKWELL and four men, reported to Central Office. Sergt. BARNETT, with three sections, was with the command under Inspector CARPENTER in the fight with the mob at Broadway and Amity. Officer DOYLE knocked down the standard-bearer, and officer THOMPSON secured the Stars and Stripes; they were subsequently presented to Inspector CARPENTER, and were borne in the center of the command. Officer RHODES was struck with a bar of iron on the head; continued the fight and was on duty until Wednesday, participating in the Twenty-second Street battle; the serious nature of the wound compelled him to retire. In the evening and until Tuesday morning the force was in reserve at Central Office.

On Tuesday morning Capt. HELME, with his command, proceeded to

the Mayor's house, in Fifth Avenue, which was being attacked; the mob
fled at the approach; a pile of bricks near the dwelling, used in some
alterations and repairs, was removed by the force to a place where they
could be of no service to a mob, and a pile, which the neighbor friends
of his Honor had placed on the stoop for defence, were also removed, so
as to be out of reach of rioters should another attack be made. Soon
after Capt. HELME, in command of his own precinct and others, was
ordered to the Second Avenue to recover arms stolen and stored in the
wire factory, corner of Twenty-second Street. The "Twenty-seventh"
was on the right; on wheeling into the avenue from Twenty-first Street
the order to charge was given, and the mob driven back, despite a desperate resistance; some fifty were placed *hors du combat,* and by the
time Twenty-second Street was reached all was clear, save the building,
which was full of rioters stealing and distributing the guns; they
were unawares caught at their work. Sergeant WILSON, with a portion
of the command, was ordered to, and at once did, rush in the building,
the rest held in front; it was five stories high. On every floor were the
ruffians busy at their work; and on every floor were they met and attacked; they fought desperately, but were driven from rooms and hall-
ways, from windows and roof-top; those who were not knocked senseless inside or killed themselves by jumping to the ground, rushed down
stairs and into the street to receive the welcome of the locusts there.
Not one man, it is thought, escaped. The rioters used in the fight the
carbines, clubbing them, but the unexpected attack prevented any successful battle; those who prostrate encumbered the building were
dragged out and left lying in the street for their friends to carry off.
The police then went to work to remove some one thousand guns; a
horse and wagon was pressed into the service, much against the owner's
will, and the weapons loaded into it. The delay caused by the work of
removing so many muskets gave an opportunity to the rioters to reas-
semble, and they did so, pouring in from all quarters above and below
on the avenue, and on Twenty-second Street. By the time the wagon
was loaded and the force in line, they were completely surrounded by an
overwhelming and infuriated mob; not a man flinched; all felt their
critical situation, but were determined to fight their way out. Just at
this juncture, when they were showered with stone and shot, and when
the mob, reinforced by that which had murdered Col. O'BRIEN, were
about rallying for an attack, Inspector DILKS, with his command of police and military, wheeled into the avenue from Twenty-first Street.
The appearance of the force was hailed by Capt. HELME's command with
the most enthusiastic cheers; the mob was assaulted in the rear, and,
staggered by the impetuosity of the charge, instantly gave way. Capt.

HELME's command joined in the fight, and soon the mob were driven in all directions. The force at once wheeled into line with Inspector DILKS' command, and accompanied him, with their spoils, in the subsequent march, incurring all the risks of what was a most hazardous tour.

In the fight at the wire factory the women were very desperate, refusing to move, and throwing stones as well as using clubs and other weapons. The men were demoniac, apparently insane with malignity and fury. After the charge into the building, officer FOLLIS was assaulted on the stairway by a man armed with a gun and a bar of iron; the fellow struck FOLLIS on the arm, badly injuring him, but was knocked senseless and disarmed. On the charge to Twenty-second Street, Roundsman WETMORE left the command and singly chased the flyers down that street, knocked down a man who was armed with a loaded pistol, taking it from him. The Captain was at the head of his men in the fight, asking no one to go where he was not willing to lead. On reaching the door of the wire factory, he wrenched a gun from the hands of the first rioter and thief rushing out, swung him to the ground, where the locusts of those among whom he had fallen did the rest.

On return to headquarters Captain HELME left for a personal inspection of his precinct. At 10 P. M. Sergeant BARNETT, who remained with force at Central Office (Sergeants WILSON and PECK, who had been until Tuesday evening with the force, being detailed to telegraph duty), went to Thirty-fourth Street and Lexington Avenue, to recover the body of the murdered Col. O'BRIEN, but it had been removed.

On Wednesday afternoon Capt. HELME and his command were returned to their own precinct; a great alarm existed in the vicinity, mobs had been visiting and threatening several buildings and hotels thereabouts. He succeeded in restoring confidence and order. Scouts in parties of four were sent out, who reported as occasion required. A number of crowds were dispersed during the night. On Wednesday P. M. the command, under Sergt. BARNETT, with Capt. HUTCHING's command, proceeded to Yorkville. Here patrol duty was performed during balance of the day and night. The next and succeeding days Sergeant BARNETT occupied himself and his command in visiting shanties and recovering stolen goods. The force recovered a very large amount. They remained in this precinct until Saturday, and then returned to their own.

On Thursday morning word was received that the colored man who had been beaten and thrown overboard from Pier No. 4, North River, was living and under the pier. Officers HEY, McCLUSKER, and DARROW, having disguised themselves as sailors, went down, hired a boat and commenced a search. At the pier, officer McCLUSKER stript, plunged in

and swam under ; after a scarch of full an hour and a half in the darkness, he found the poor fellow crouching on the stone-work, nearly naked,
all blood and half insane; he had a large stone clutched in his hand ; it
was a long while before the officer could convince him he was a friend
and come to rescue him, but finally succeeded ; this accomplished, Mc-
Clusker swam out and had the boat rowed under ; the alarm of the
negro was again aroused, and it was almost by main force that he was
got into the boat.   The three manly-hearted officers then rowed with
him to the police-boat No. 1, near by, where he was taken on board and
kindly cared for.

Saturday evening Sergt. Barnett, having returned from Yorkville
with Roundsman Rigney and Fourth Section, reported at the Central
Office, and next (Sunday) morning went with Capt. Dickson to Hastings,
Dobbs' Ferry, Tarrytown, and Sing Sing.   The particulars of this expedition will be given in the record of the Twenty-ninth.   They were
on this expedition three days, and did ably and cheerfully all the duties
consequent upon it.

Sergt. M. B. Wilson was left alone in the station on the morning of
the Riot Week.   A colored man was brought in for safety, and the station
was at once the object of the mob's attention.   The Sergeant closed and
barricaded the doors, and awaited an attack.   The mob cooled off and
left, and the negro was sent away in safety.   Officer Carroll was, while
reconnoitering at Liberty and Greenwich Streets, twice knocked down
by a mob, but escaped without serious injury.   When the Captain returned temporarily to his own precinct, on Tuesday, he heard of a
mob attacking a man who was mistaken for one Smith, the proprietor of
a drinking house in Greenwich Street.   The house of this Smith had,
the night before, been attacked and sacked, and he had shot a party whom
he considered among those engaged, killing him on the spot, and then
escaped.   The man attacked was one of his cmployes.   Capt. Helme
and officer Carroll repaired to the scene and succeeded in rescuing the
man, who was quite severely injured.   On Wednesday, Thursday and
Friday nights, officers Carroll, Hey, and McClusker were on scouting
duty, in citizens' dress, throughout the precinct—a duty of no little hazard, and, as they performed it, of great value.   Sergeant Barnett attracted the attention of his officers and men, as he did the attention of
the Commissioners and Superintendents, during the entire week of the
riots, by his unwearying activity, his indomitable courage, and his manly,
intelligent performance of all duties.   There was nothing required of
him that was not thoroughly performed.   He is literally a noble fellow
and excellent officer.   The more such men as Barnett the higher
the repute of the force.

The services of this force were of an almost constant and certainly arduous and hazardous character.   They did faithfully and manfully all duties which they were called on to perform, and have placed themselves in an honorable light before the higher officers of the Department and the public.

Twenty-eighth Precinct.

Captain JOHN F. DICKSON, No. 550 Greenwich Street.   In the morning of Monday Sergeant WOLFE and ten men were ordered to report to Captain SPEIGHT, at Marshal's office, No. 1190 Broadway, but finding the office closed, and no one to report to, repaired to Fortieth Street and Third Avenue, in which vicinity it was heard a riot was raging.   On reaching Third Avenue from Forty-third Street, meantime being joined by more police, a charge was made on the mob, which, fighting desperately, was driven back to and beyond Forty-sixth Street, where they broke. The rioters seemed seized with terror at the determined character of the charge, and fled in all directions ; the entire force did not exceed fifty —their opponents thousands—and the punishment inflicted was of the most severe character, the rioters laying thick as the force advanced ; the force had penetrated to the front of the Marshal's office at Forty-sixth Street, which was in flames, but received no support, the police which had been on the ground having been beaten off.   The mob rallied, hurled themselves upon the Twenty-eighth and their associates, and in a brief time broke them, every man looking out for himself ; stones and brickbats and shot were showered on them like hail, and, in the close pursuit, clubs fell upon them with damaging effect.   Some ran into dwellings, were secreted, subsequently escaping in disguise ; others ran the gauntlet of the guns, clubs, and missiles, but all reported as soon as possible after the disaster to the station.

In this battle, officer DAPKE, on the retreat, was seriously injured, but got away, and was secreted in a dwelling ; officer HOLLEY had a finger broken ; officer SIEBERT was set upon by a number of men, and his arm broken ; officers POLHAMUS, BRYAN, and BASSFORD had severe scalp wounds ; officer KNIGHT was badly injured in the chest, and Sergeant WOLFE, who was the last to retreat, had to fight his way out, and was badly injured on the head.   Officers KNIGHT and BOLMAN were saved by some women, who afforded them refuge in their houses, whence they escaped in disguise.

At 11.40 A. M. Roundsman MANGLES reported, with eleven men, to Capt. PORTER, Forty-sixth Street and Third Avenue ; had been there but a short time ere the mob made an overwhelming charge, scattering the force in all directions.   Capt. PORTER, unwilling to sacrifice his men, gave the order to retreat, and it was wise that he did so; he saved many valuable lives.   This force of the precinct reported as soon as possible after the defeat to Capt. DICKSON, at the station.

In the afternoon Capt. DICKSON, with Sergeants O'CONNOR and GROAT, reported at the Central Office.   In the evening they were under the command of Inspector CARPENTER in the crushing of the mob in the Park, and their locusts flew well and effectively.   Sergeant O'CONNOR had his head badly cut here, and was compelled to retire from duty.   All through the Fourth Precinct were they with the Inspector, moving the mobs from pillar to post, eventually dispersing all of them and restoring order to a section which was alive with riot and pillage.   On return to Central Office, were held in reserve until Tuesday A. M., when, at 2 o'clock, they accompanied Sergeant COPELAND to Clarkson Street, where the body of the murdered negro was recovered.   Soon after ordered to the fire at the packing-house, corner Houston and Washington Streets, where they remained till 5 A. M.; thence to Leroy Street, where Capt. DICKSON rescued the negro who had been knocked down by a crowd, and beaten on the head by a rioter, with a stone weighing twenty pounds, until he was thought dead.   This fiend stood over the poor fellow when he laid on the street, deliberately lifted and brought down the stone upon his head five or six times, gritting his teeth, yelling his execrations, and reveling in his cowardly and hellish deed of blood.   The negro, in defending himself before this, had knocked his murderer down several times.   The rioter had fled from him, leaving it to a score of others to render him defenceless, and, when the poor fellow was insensible, he returned to complete the work of murder.   Capt. DICKSON pressed into service a wagon, and, putting the sufferer into it, conveyed him to the hospital.   No horse could be had, and the men turned in, drawing the wagon.   The poor fellow died soon after, but meantime was able to whisper his name—WILLIAMS—to the Captain.   Three persons charged with the murder have since been arrested by this force.

On Tuesday, at 10.30 A. M., Capt. DICKSON and his command were, under Inspector DILKS, of those who visited the factory where stolen arms were stored at Twenty-second Street and Second Avenue.   The Twenty-eighth Precinct had the right.   Inspector DILKS' command drove, it will be remembered, after severe fighting, the mob before them, then entered, and took the well-defended building, and recovered a large number of arms.   It was one of the most severe fights of the entire campaign, and thoroughly tested the "mettle" of the police.   Sergeant GROAT had a desperate encounter with a well-armed, courageous, and muscular fellow; he fought him, with reckless courage, some two hundred yards up the

avenue and away from the command, but succeeded in bringing him to
the ground; on the running fight the fellow turned, and a blow on the
back of his head produced the phenomenon of a full set of teeth flying out
of his mouth, and pirouetting in the air, falling some ten feet distant;
they were evidently false, as was the heart of the fellow wearing them.
In this battle not one innocent man was punished, but the avenue was
literally strewn with the bodies of the rioters.   Many were picked up
and hastily removed; carried off, no one knows and few care where, and
others were carried to their homes to live or die, as the nature of their
wounds permitted.

So soon as returned to Central Office, Capt. DICKSON and his command were ordered to report to Inspector LEONARD, at City Hall, and
were on guard in Printing-house Square and Park, doing active and
valuable duty in preventing concentration of inflamed and inflammatory
crowds.   They remained here until Saturday, Inspector LEONARD bearing cheerful testimony to their vigilance and efficiency, when they were
returned to their own precinct.

On Sunday morning this precinct, with others, Capt. DICKSON in
command, were detailed to visit the different villages and towns up the
river so far as Peekskill.   They were accompanied by Companies A and
B, Seventy-fourth Regiment New York Volunteers, of Buffalo, Lieut.
NAGLE in command, and were everywhere received with the utmost enthusiasm.   Residents threw open their houses to them, and volunteered
every hospitality.   Capt. DICKSON in most cases declined, because of the
numbers of his command, and his hesitancy in accepting hospitalities
which, however well meant, might prove onerous.   The force were gone
until Wednesday, the 22d, disembarking *en route* and on return at every
place, restoring confidence and assuring the residents of protection and
assistance.   Capt. DICKSON and his command speak in glowing terms of
Lieut. NAGLE and his command of the Seventy-fourth Regiment.   Fresh
from the duties of the war and noble service, their time had expired on Saturday, but they at once *volunteered* for the expedition.   During it they won
the admiration and respect of the citizens of every place visited, by their
manly bearing and deportment.   They co-operated cordially with the
police, emulated them in considerate conduct at all places visited, and,
while they proved themselves soldiers, proved also that they were gallant and chivalrous gentlemen.

On the return of the force they had but a brief respite, for, on Thursday, Capt. DICKSON was ordered to Port Richmond.   Reaching there he
marched to Quarantine; thence to Vanderbilt's Landing.   Here the riot
had occurred in which two citizens had been killed; he marched his
command through all the infected section, meeting with none but peace-

able demonstrations; the force during the day had marched eleven miles under a burning sun; two were prostrated and carried back to the boat. At 5 P. M. the command returned to New York. On reaching the dock they were met with orders to go to Flushing, L. I., and were joined by Lieut. BIRD and company, Seventh Regiment, who were in waiting. Off at once they went, arriving at 8½ P. M., landed, marched through the village, and, finding all quiet, returned to the boat. Here they remained all night, and, in the morning, after another tour through the village, returned to the city, arriving at 3 P. M. Well fagged out, the force marched to its own precinct.

No force had more arduous and more prolonged duties than the "Twenty-eighth," and from first to last every call upon Capt. DICKSON and his command was obeyed with alacrity. In every engagement to which they were parties they evinced the utmost courage, and their escutcheon is unstained by a single unworthy act. For a week and a half they were on constant duty, and have won full honors by the manner in which all requirements were performed. To Capt. DICKSON, whose example and endurance encouraged his men, the greatest credit is due. Sergeant WILLIAM GROAT and detective HENRY JAY, during the entire period of service, were unwearying, active, and courageous. Sergeant VAN DEUSEN was left in charge of the station. On two occasions he was threatened by the mob, but coolly prepared for them, and, with but four men, not only managed to save the building, but the refugees in it. In the battle on the Second Avenue, under Inspector DILKS, one of this force disposed of four of the worst of the rioters. He went into the fight on his own hook. His favorite cry was, when he brought a villain down. "Hallo! Johnny Roach, how *are* you?"

Twenty-ninth Precinct.

Capt. F. C. SPEIGHT, East Twenty-ninth Street, near Fourth Avenue. Except when detailed in squads, the Twenty-ninth was always under the immediate command of the Captain. Saturday, before the riot, Sergt. VAN ORDEN, with fifteen men, took charge of the Seventh Avenue Arsenal, remaining until Monday afternoon. Many manifestations were made against the building, but the force determined to defend it to the last. Early on Monday Capt. SPEIGHT, with twenty men, reported at the Marshal's Office, No. 1190 Broadway, where the drafting proceeded quietly until adjournment at noon. Capt. SPEIGHT withdrew his men at 4 P. M. having, during his stay, dispersed several crowds, and reported at Central Office. Ten minutes after he left, the mob reassembled, and the Marshal's Office was in flames. The entire block from Twenty-eighth to

Twenty-ninth Street was destroyed.   During the morning word was received that Superintendent KENNEDY had been killed, and Capt. SPEIGHT,
without waiting for orders, sent off Sergt. YOUNG with a force to the
Nineteenth Ward to recover him ; meantime he had been rescued.   On
Monday evening the entire command was with Inspector CARPENTER in
the Park, and were active participants in the battle there with those who
had attempted to fire the *Tribune* Buildings.   Subsequently were with
Inspector CARPENTER in the tour through the Fourth Ward and in the
several engagements ; in this section houses occupied by colored people
had been fired from below, driving the inmates up stairs, whose only
escape was by jumping into the street ; some of them were clinging to
window-sills, some to the eaves, and the clothes of some, while thus suspended, had caught fire.   The police did all in their power to rescue
them, but in many instances, for want of ladders, were unable to.   A number were, in falling, seriously injured, and one killed.   Thence Captain
SPEIGHT and command were ordered to Inspector LEONARD's command
at City Hall, and were constantly on the different expeditions of the night.
Officer O'BYRNE was attacked in Chatham Street, near the Park, his club
wrenched from him and he badly beaten with it; he recovered the locust,
fought his men, and succeeded in bringing one into the Twenty-sixth Precinct station-house, who was in a condition which required immediate
attention of the surgeon.   This fellow's name was DERMOTT; he was
afterwards sent to the City Hospital, but escaped on Wednesday.

Tuesday morning reported to Inspector CARPENTER, at Central Office,
and with his command marched to Second Avenue and Thirty-fourth
Street.   Capt. SPEIGHT and command were on the rear, and upon this
portion of the battalion an attack was made on the avenue soon after
passing above Thirty-fourth street.   From the streets and houses shots
and missiles of all kinds were poured thick and fast ; Capt. SPEIGHT at
once faced the rear ranks about, and ordered a charge on the mob closing
up from below.   But the men were momentarily staggered and bewildered by the sudden and desperate character of the attack ; Capt. SPEIGHT
had on giving the word dashed ahead, and was far in advance, the target
for hundreds, when he was knocked down with a brick.   His fall recovered the men, and they came on with a rush.   The Captain was on his
feet ere they reached him, and joined in an onslaught on the mob.   The
clubs fell mercilessly, and men fell under them.   The mob were beaten
and fled.   Meantime the fire from the houses continued.   Inspector CAR-
PENTER sent orders from the front to charge, take, and clear them.   On
went the force to the work.   The houses were stormed and entered, and
cleared, from the cellar to the roof, of every one save women and children,
and those whom Capt. SPEIGHT, from a prior Captaincy in that vicinity,

knew to be peaceable men.   The fighting inside was of the severest character, the rioters well armed, and fighting for their lives.   Few of them,
if any, escaped without serious injury.   In GRAHAM'S liquor store, corner
Thirty-fourth Street and Second Avenue, eight or ten rioters had fallen
and lay wedged in between the liquor casks.   Although the houses were
filled with women and children—many of the former urging the men
on to their riotous work—not one of either was hurt; the children were
carried by the officers out of harm's way.   Roundsman ROBERTS carried
three little ones, placing them in rooms where they would be safe from
danger and out of sight of the painful scenes.

Capt. SPEIGHT in one of the houses met an old man on the stairs : " For
God's sake, Captain, save my life !"   A rioter above aimed a blow at the
Captain, but it would have struck the old man had not SPEIGHT caught it
on his own arm.   He placed the old gentleman in a place of safety, and
hurried up stairs; in one room saw a woman with her crinoline well
spread out, sitting in a corner; she asked him to save her child, and he
carried it to another room for safety; returning queried of her what she
had behind her, and compelling her to remove, a lusty, fierce looking
fellow, with club in hand, was revealed ; a brisk combat ensued, but the
rioter fared the worst and was sent down stairs to the mercies of those
below.   On one floor a woman was in the hall holding a door to prevent
the man within from getting out; the Captain removed her, and from the
room sprang a fellow making an onslaught with his club, but striking
wild in his frenzy ; soon down stairs he went, not to return again.   The
work of clearing being complete, the force—this was the battle of the
rear ranks—reformed and joined the balance of the command.   This was
considered one of the sharpest engagements of the campaign.   The force
engaged suffered considerably, but it was estimated that over thirty of
the rioters were seriously punished.

After returning to Central Office, Capt. SPEIGHT and command reported to Inspector LEONARD at City Hall, where they remained all
night; were engaged in the different tours of the Fourth, Fifth, and
Eighth Wards, and in the divers skirmishes with, and dispersal of, the
mobs.   On Wednesday morning, reported to the Central Office, from
whence they were almost unceasingly engaged in expeditions and special
duties until Saturday, when ordered to their own precinct.   This force
numbers thirty men more than any other, and, consequently, were always in demand and performed extra duty.   "Fall in, Twenty-ninth,"
became a by-word, so constantly was the order given.

Sergeants VAN ORDEN and YOUNG were active in the service.   Sergeant WARD was very ill, but reported himself before expiration of leave
for duty, and was assigned to care of the station, relieving Sergt. JONES,

who had been ill for a long while. The station-house was made the hospital for policemen and others for the upper portion of the city. Fourteen of the Twenty-ninth had been severely injured, one since dead and two yet in hospital. The Captain also received a severe injury on the leg, from which he will long be a sufferer. Surgeon GRISCOM was unwearying and skillful in his attentions to all the injured.

The labor of this precinct was uninterrupted for five days and nights. Capt. SPEIGHT is a bold and valuable officer, a veteran in the matter of handling mobs, and he had, in the devotion to duty of his men, their bravery and willingness to respond to any call, a force which made them of signal service.

Thirtieth Precinct.

Capt. J. HARTT, One Hundred and Thirty-first Street, Manhattanville. On Monday the whole force of this precinct was held in reserve, and on Tuesday morning reported at Central Office. At noon were returned to their own precinct, where disturbances were apprehended, and where numerous dwellings had been threatened. Capt. HARTT, soon as reaching his station, made admirable arrangements for preservation of peace and property, so disposing his force as to be able to use them effectively. After their return there were no violent demonstrations, the rioters in that section evidently not caring to come into collision with them. One of the dwellings which had been especially threatened, the Captain, with a force, took charge of, remaining there till apprehensions no longer existed. Meantime, intimations were given that his own would be burned, but he said that his first duty was to the public, and that he had not force enough to spare any to look after his own interests. The family of the house he was protecting had left; when asked by a body of rioters what he intended to do, he said he intended to fight, and to give the Coroner, if it was made necessary, more jobs in a day than he had had in a year. The determined conduct of the force had the best effect in cooling down the riotously disposed. Special protection was afforded several dwellings, beside the one above referred to, and there is no doubt that but for the return of the force, this precinct would have been the scene of arson and pillage to a great extent. Although the Thirtieth had no opportunity to participate in the more active and exciting scenes of the week, they were of the first importance in their own precinct, and have the acknowledgment of the inhabitants for their valuable and intelligent services.

On Tuesday night Sergeant BLAKE was in charge of the station-house, with two sick officers; a mob passed, but did nothing more than throw a few stones. While the force were away, on Tuesday, two men, armed, drove around notifying certain residents—among them the Captain's family—to move out, for on Wednesday the dwellings would be burned down. The appearance of the force, as shown, however, put a stop both to threats and consummation. A few of the riots in which Capt. HARTT has had a schooling, are the 'Long-shore, the Riot of 1857, and the famous Bone Riot. The experience gained in these and others would have operated badly for the lawless had they evoked it.

Thirty-first Precinct.

Capt. James Z. BOGART, Eighty-sixth Street, Bloomingdale Road. On Monday a portion of the force held in reserve at their own station, and a portion under the Captain, with Sergts. TEN EYCK and BARRETT, reported at Central Office, remained until Tuesday morning, when the command, with others, under Inspector CARPENTER, marched to Second Avenue and Thirty-fourth Street. The fight and capture of the houses here by the rear ranks, of which the Thirty-first were one, has been described in the record of the "Twenty-ninth." Capt. BOGART and his men were in the buildings, and had many a hand-to-hand encounter, never flinching from their work, but doing it manfully—zealously. Sergt. TEN EYCK and officers THOMPSON, STEVENSON, and STODDARD, were especially noticeable during this exciting affair for the courage they displayed. Indeed, the force, none of them, evaded any hazard, but performed their duty vigorously and thoroughly, as many of the victims of their locusts will, if they can at all, regretfully testify. This force was also, of course, under the heavy fire from the houses and the street, and were a portion of those assailing and beating the mob on the avenue. After return to Central Office, they were ordered to Inspector DILKS' command, which, at Twenty-second Street and Second Avenue, had such a severe fight. Here the mob were vastly superior in numbers, were well armed, and well contested the charge made upon them. It was a close fight, the crowd falling back slowly at first, but the persistent locusts were dropping upon them with telling effect, and when they did break, it was in terror and confusion. Their wounded laid along the street, and many were promptly cared for by the women, but the most of them were not attended to or moved until the force had left the ground.

In the evening Capt. BOGART, in charge of a force, including his own command, and a body of military, visited the Sixteenth Ward; a crowd was dispersed from Mr. GIBBONS' house in Twenty-ninth Street, near Eighth Avenue, the command moving on. No sooner were they out of sight than the rioters rallied, broke into the house, having stoned the front

almost to ruin, and commenced sacking it. Capt. Bogart had not
marched far ere he heard of this, and at once took his command back ; a
portion of the rioters were caught in the street, but a large number in
the house.   A charge to the front produced the speedy flight of the
rioters in the street, and then a portion of the force were ordered into the
building.   Nearly everything that could be carried had been taken away;
closets, trunks, and drawers had been broken open and general pillage
had been the order.   Parties were at work when the police entered ;
they were caught in the halls, parlors, on the stairways, and in the chambers, each ladened; the men thieves were shown no mercy, but received
their full deserts.   In order not to encumber the house a number were
hauled out to the sidewalk.   On this occasion it was, when a number
of police were engaged on and about the stoop with the thieves who
came rushing out, that the military fired without orders, wounding six
of the police, one fatally and others seriously, and riddling one of the
rioters with balls; subsequently, some of the military made a charge,
one of the thieves being transfixed with bayonets.   The punishments
here were among the most severe the rioters, in proportion to their
numbers, anywhere received.   Not much of property was recovered, the
sacking having been done in a remarkably short time.   So soon as the
house was broken into it was literally filled with men and boys,
women and girls; some of the women fought the police savagely.

On return to Central Office, the force were in reserve until Wednesday, when it returned to its own precinct to meet emergencies there,
doing special duty until Saturday, but without having to suppress any
disturbances.

This force were in the two severe battles in Second Avenue, and in
the disastrous one, so far as injury to the police was concerned, at
Mr. Gibbons' house.   They were well tested as to courage, endurance,
and discipline, and sustained themselves bravely, being important auxil-
iaries in the suppression of the riots and the restoration of order.   The
quiet in their own precinct, which was likely to be disturbed just about
the time they returned, was preserved by the judicious management of
Capt. Bogart and the faithfulness with which all orders were promptly
and thoroughly obeyed.

Thirty-second Precinct.

Capt. A. S. Wilson, Fort Washington.   The Captain and his force reported at Central Office on Tuesday morning, with Sergts. Huff, White-
man, and Castle, coming down by Hudson River Railroad; were soon
after *en route*, with Inspector Dilks' command, to Twenty-second Street

and Second Avenue, where the mob was driven off, the building in which stolen arms were secreted entered, and a general clubbing given to the lawless outside and in the building. The "Thirty-second" were active and gallant in this affair, and seemed to relish infantry duty after their uninterrupted duty as mounted police. Returning to headquarters, there was but a brief respite ere again, under Inspector DILKS, they marched to the same vicinity, engaged in another conflict, where their command was again conspicuous, and were parties to another victory. It was at this time that Capt. HELME's command was being hemmed in from all quarters, and its safety, bravely as his men would have fought, was largely due to the opportune arrival of Inspector DILKS. The hazardous return march, and the stubborn persistence of the mob in their assaults, have already been fully described. On reaching headquarters Capt. WILSON and his command were sent through the infected districts of the Eleventh and Seventeenth Wards, and on return reported to Inspector LEONARD at the City Hall; from here, aside of the day duties, were sent at night to the Western Hotel, and had a hand in the dispersion of the mob which had threatened it, several of the parties being cracked on the head somewhat severely; thence to Cedar Street, and the Government Stores; to the Twenty-seventh Precinct, and a march through it, and, 4 A. M. Wednesday, after nearly twenty-four hours of continuous march, interrupted only to give battle, returned to the City Hall, and stretching out on the marble floor the members were allowed a brief rest. On Tuesday night the men had a short respite, and the Captain found them a genuine friend in Mr. CROOK, of Chatham Street. On hearing that they had been nearly all day without food, he aroused his servants, opened his establishment, and had the force brought in, furnishing them with an excellent, substantial, and, of course, most welcome repast. They resolved him to be a whole-souled man.

On Wednesday, at 3 P. M., Capt. WILSON and his command were ordered to the First Precinct Station-house, and thence proceeded to Pier No. 4, North River, dispersing a crowd there; subsequently the vicinity was patroled, and quiet entirely restored. Soon after, in consequence of apprehensions at Carmansville, they were ordered there. They arrived at Fort Washington by boat at 6½ P. M. The Captain at once took a force and started for Carmansville, where a large number of people were met, threatening mischief. He used "moral suasion" with them in preference to the locust, as they did not appear to be of a very vicious class, and they soon dispersed. The force were kept together until Sunday A. M., but had no disturbances to subdue.

Sergeant FLANDREAU was left in charge of the station-house, having under his command one officer, two doormen, and two hostlers. On Tuesday, when the force had left for Central Office, a number of ladies and gentlemen residing at Carmansville, Fort Washington, and Tubby Hook, came to the station, and expressed their fears in regard to the destruction of their dwellings; the gentlemen offered their services. Sergeant FLANDREAU allayed their apprehensions. At night he dispatched Patrolman CROSBY and Doorman MALONE on different reconnoitering duties, which they did most faithfully. Fresh horses were constantly kept on hand, and the few men at his disposal were actively scouting. When not doing this, they made a bold front at the station, demeaning themselves as though the whole force were on hand, and could be brought at once into service. During the night a man living in the neighborhood, one of doubtful character, repeatedly reconnoitered the station, and was inquisitive as to the number of men and the means of defence and offence. He received discreet answers and communicated them to a gang ready for arson and pillage, who thereupon skedaddled. On Wednesday, during the morning, the Sergeant was run down with the terrified residents of the vicinity; he endeavored to allay their fears, told them how thoroughly the precinct had been patroled, but all in vain so far as a large number were concerned, who packed up their valuables and removed with their families to Westchester County. Confident of his own ability, with his few men and the volunteer force he could raise, to preserve order, yet the alarm and absquatulating induced the Sergeant to telegraph for Capt. WILSON and his force. Their return on Wednesday was the signal for a general jubilation. They arrived just in time to check the crowd at Carmansville, above referred to.

This force, although from the " rural districts," were most active in duty. They performed an immense amount of labor, were in some of the worst fights of the Riot Week, and exhibited au endurance, fidelity, and courage which covers them with credit. Capt. WILSON never sought for himself or men rest or respite; and every one of the force, from Capt. WILSON down, were up to every requirement promptly and cheerfully. Sergeant FLANDREAU also won honor by his cool, discreet course, while left alone in the precinct, and which, undoubtedly, prevented demonstrations by the inhabitants so dreaded.

The Sanitary Police.

The Sanitary Police, Capt. B. G. LORD, Rooms Nos. 37 and 38 Central Office, have as their especial duties the reporting of all nuisances, examination of tenement houses, and of unsafe buildings, the care of the Public Schools, but, more especially and important, the examination of steam boilers and the licensing of persons qualified to run steam-engines.

This last it will be seen involves the intelligent and scientific examination of parties applicant, and, as a consequence, the force is composed in large proportion of scientific men.   Their duties, although not constantly before the public, are of a most responsible character, and have been most competently performed.   During "Riot Week" their ordinary routine was broken, and they were most valuable aids in the restoration of order.

The Sanitary Company was called to the Central Office, on Monday afternoon, July 13 ; in the evening, with the force under Inspector CAR-PENTER, proceeded to Printing-house Square, and also patroled through a portion of the Fourth Ward ; returning to Central Office, were in reserve during the balance of the night.

On Tuesday morning Captain LORD and company proceeded to Prince and Crosby Streets and dispersed a large collection of rioters assembled with the intention of burning a colored church situated at that corner.   On the return to Central Office, they were ordered to the factory at Twenty-second Street and Second Avenue.   The force sent on this expedition (which was the first attack made on the rioters at that point) numbered about two hundred regular policemen, under the command of Inspector G. W. DILKS, who led them on through Twenty-first Street ; on arriving at the corner of Twenty-first Street and Second Avenue, the order of double-quick was given, when the whole force charged up to and through the mob and on the building ; forced the doors, and found the stairs leading to the upper floors filled with rioters armed with carbines, which they used as clubs.   A portion of the command were ordered to enter the building and get to the rear of the rioters, which was done after hard fighting, and as they were driven out they were compelled to run the gauntlet through the force outside, but few escaping. Each one of the command secured a carbine, and on the order being given to fall in, they returned to the Central Office.   After the return, the Sanitary Company were again dispatched under command of Inspector CAR-PENTER, with Capt. LORD as aid, accompanied by about one hundred and fifty police and a detachment of military, to patrol the Seventeenth Ward. On their return officers McTAGGART and JAQUINS were detailed to accompany a detachment of police, under command of Capt. BOGART, and a company of Regulars under command of Capt. FRANKLIN.   This force proceeded in eleven stages, and the above-named officers were ordered to take charge of the drivers, many of whom had refused to drive through the crowds of rioters.   The stages having stopped on the corner of Thirtieth Street and Eighth Avenue, while the military and police proceeded down Twenty-ninth Street toward Tenth Avenue, the officers left in charge of them were in imminent danger of being attacked ; but they flinched not ; and, on being ordered to take the stages over to the Fifth Avenue and

Twenty-ninth Street and await the coming of the police and military, they started on the perilous trip; although attacked with stones and other missiles by the mob, they succeeded in reaching that point, and were joined by the force.

The Sanitary Company were held at the Central Office until Wednesday morning, when a portion of it, with the entire force of the Twelfth Precinct, accompanied by Capt. FRANKLIN's Regulars, were ordered to Harlem, where there had been riotous demonstrations during the absence of the police. On Wednesday night they assisted in arresting a number of rioters who had assembled to fire the house of some colored people residing in One Hundred and Twenty-second Street. They patroled the precinct through the night. On Thursday morning officer JAMES MONT-GOMERY, of the Sanitary, assisted by a portion of the Company then at Harlem, arrested a party charged with riot, arson and highway robbery. On the same morning a portion of the company arrested, in his place of business, a person accused of aiding and abetting the rioters, and inciting them to burn the house of Mr. EDGAR KETCHUM, collector of Internal Revenue for the Government.

On Thursday night the Company, and members of the Twelfth Precinct, patroled the precinct. On Friday they proceeded with some prisoners, whom they had assisted in arresting at Mott Haven previously, and took them to Melrose, where they were committed to await their trial. The stable of ABRAHAM BROWN, City Marshal, on 124th Street, was fired on this day; the force was promptly on the spot and the flames speedily extinguished. On Saturday evening the portion of the Sanitary Company at Harlem returned to the Central Office.

On Wednesday afternoon, after a portion of his Company had been ordered to Harlem, Capt. LORD, with the balance of the Sanitary Company and other force, was ordered to take charge of the Sixteenth Precinct. After his arrival, he deputized about one hundred and fifty citizens as special policemen, who, with the police under his command, patroled the precinct. During the command of Captain LORD in the Sixteenth Precinct, there were several attempts at arson, which were frustrated by the vigilance of the men, and only one fire occurred, which was immediately extinguished by the Fire Department, aided by the force. On Saturday, after having returned to the Central Office, and his whole Company (the Sanitary) being again together, he was intrusted with the charge and protection of the Central Office, which duty the Company fulfilled day and night until Monday the 27th July. During the guard of the Central Office, officers JOHNS, VAN ORDEN, and McTAGGART, arrested three persons charged with entering the house of ISAAC STEPHENS (colored) and beating him. Officer McTAGGART arrested a man charged with assault on colored persons. Officers COFFEE and VAN ORDEN arrested three others for assault and battery on three soldiers stationed at the Central Office.

On Monday, July 27, the Sanitary Company returned to their regular duties. On Monday morning, July 13, about 10 A. M., officer McTAGGART was present at the riot and burning of the buildings on Third Avenue and Forty-sixth Street. There saw Superintendent KENNEDY beaten by the mob, and assisted in his rescue from them. While Mr. KENNEDY was being taken away, McTAGGART was struck with a stone in the back of his head, and also with a club on the shoulder. He aided in conveying the Superintendent to headquarters. On Monday afternoon, as the same officer was in an office in West Thirty-ninth Street, he heard one of the persons present boast that he had taken a prominent part in the mobs' proceedings of the day, and that they intended to burn several slaughter-houses and ALLERTON's Hotel. The man also stated that he would put a ball through HENRY ALBOHN, who has since died from the effects of a pistol-shot wound. The jury subsequently convened at the inquest charged this man with the murder of ALBOHN, and he was arrested by officer McTAGGART, and committed for trial.

This force, as will be noticed, performed miscellaneous and prolonged duty, "fleshed their locusts," and encountered perils in common with others of the Department. Capt. LORD, ever zealous and possessing moral courage which is infectious, incited his men, and was emulated by them, to a full performance of duty and the attaining of a most honorable name upon the "Record."

DRILL-OFFICER T. S. COPELAND.

Sergeant T. S. COPELAND, whose services as drill-officer to the force have been of the utmost value, was one of the most efficient of the officers during Riot Week. His first duty was organizing the command of Inspector CARPENTER, which, on Monday afternoon, met the mob at Broadway and Amity Street, and he had the second blow in what was a gallant fight, and a quick and complete victory. It was here that the police, by their bravery, extorted from the citizens gathered at the spot, cheer on cheer of approval—something unusual for the force to hear given them, but which will be nothing novel hereafter. This mob was the one which had been doing so much damage in the upper part of the city, and they came down ladened with plunder. In the evening Sergeant COPELAND formed another large command, which, under Inspector CARPENTER, marched to the Park, and gave the rioters fleeing from Printing-house Square a reception such as they little expected, and largely suffered from. The Sergeant was here also amongst the most

conspicuous and foremost.   Thence he was on the march through the
Fourth Ward.   Here were witnessed shocking scenes; the sacking of
houses occupied by negroes, the piling up and burning of their furniture,
the firing of their dwellings, and, in some cases, the actual burning
alive of the inmates.   In one instance a dwelling was fired where seven
negroes had taken refuge; they escaped by jumping from the windows, a
distance of twenty feet; one broke his leg, another his arm, and it was
only by the prompt and decisive action of the police that any of them
escaped death, the mob standing ready, like so many wolves, to jump
upon them the moment they reached the ground.   In this march the
various mobs were met and dispersed, the greater portion fleeing back
into their dens.   At midnight the force returned to the Park in time to
receive the large mob coming down Broadway to finish the interrupted
work at the *Tribune* Building.   It was here that Inspector CARPENTER
exhibited strategy and generalship, massing his force at the east side of
the Park, and, covered by the darkness, coolly awaiting the mob which
came on, singing "We'll hang old GREELEY to a sour apple tree," and
rushed into the grasp of the force ere their presence was suspected.
Exemplary, sudden, thorough was their punishment after the force
sprang upon them.   "Up, Guards, and at them," was the word; the song
ceased, and the ringing of the locusts and cries for mercy of the rene-
gades supplied its place.   Here, too, was Sergeant COPELAND brave
and efficient.   Returning to headquarters, but a brief respite was had,
for, at 2 A. M., Tuesday, Sergeant C. formed a battalion of 100 men, and
proceeded to Clarkson Street, to recover the body of the negro hung
there.   It was recovered and brought to the Central Office.   On Tues
day the Sergeant formed the battalion of police which, under Inspector CARPENTER, visited Second Avenue and Thirty-fourth Street,
where the severe battle, heretofore described, was had.   The force used
their revolvers to clear the tops of the houses of their assailants, but ultimately had to charge the houses, take and "clean" them.   The rioters
most of them boldly met the assault, others were found secreted in beds,
boxes, closets, &c., &c., but were hunted out, receiving lessons which
those of them who can remember anything, are not likely to forget.   The
force returned to headquarters at noon, and during the balance of the
day the military knowledge of the Sergeant was in constant requisition
in the organizing of the different commands constantly being required
and sent off.   In the evening he was with the command which, under
Inspector CARPENTER, marched to BROOKS BROTHERS' clothing store, and
subsequently through the infected districts thereabouts, dispersing all
mobs and administering, on several occasions, severe punishment; thence
to the Fifth Ward, where valuable service was done and quiet restored,

and thence to headquarters.   During the balance of the week, until Saturday, Sergeant COPELAND was occupied in organizing companies, as they were required, for special service.

In hastily giving a record of the duties and doings of this officer we have omitted many instances connected therewith, but which have been given in connection with the record of divers precincts.   His conduct had elicited the hearty encomiums of his superior officers, and he was not only valuable because of his military knowledge and the promptness and ability with which he formed commands, but also as a cool, gallant, and faithful officer.

The Honorable Record would be incomplete without reference to three gentlemen—DANIEL B. HASBROUCK, First Deputy Clerk; GEORGE HOPCRAFT, Clerk to Superintendent; and HORACE A. BLISS, Clerk to Inspectors.   The two former, during Riot Week, were occupied day and night, unceasingly, in the performance of varied duties, neither of them making note of hours or weariness, but lending their whole time and energies to the intelligent and valuable services they were called upon to perform.   When the immense amount of business centralizing at headquarters, and the responsible character of what devolved on them to do, is remembered, that they were the right men in the right places will be promptly and cheerfully conceded.   Mr. BLISS was temporarily absent at the burial of a brother, but returned in time to make available to the department the intelligence and energy which he is so well known to possess.

ALEXANDER STEWART, Messenger to the Inspectors, was among the faithful and unwearying during the period of unceasing work and excitement.

The Brooklyn Precincts.

There are ten Precincts in Brooklyn.   The force is a portion of the the Metropolitan Police.   Its movements in this city on the first day of the riots is detailed in the Record of its own Chief officer, Inspector FOLK, herein given, as are also the valuable duties subsequently performed in Brooklyn.   That city owes its exemption to the constant vigilance of the force, its intelligent and courageous action.

Conclusion.

In concluding the " Honorable Record " of the Metropolitan Police, it can be reiterated that the safety of the city, its exemption from unprecedented scenes of murder, arson, and pillage was first due to the force. It should be borne in mind that of the 2,000 men composing it, the Commissioners at no one time could avail themselves of over 800, and on Monday of the outbreak of not more than half that number. The balance, on reporting at headquarters, were sent in detachments to all sections of the city ; and to some precincts it was found necessary not only to return its force but to strengthen them with others ; nor were the 800 available in a body, for they were being constantly sent off under different commands to attack mobs in diverse sections of the city. The largest number in one command was 350.

It is a noticeable fact that, in every engagement where the police were *in force*, they were victorious ; it mattered not how many they had to meet or how they had to meet them— whether in the streets or in houses, or in both at once ; on all occasions they were entirely successful. This result is due to what very many citizens have considered an unnecessary regulation of the Department, and which many of the force have objected to as onerous, annoying and useless. We refer to the drilling and disciplining of the men, which has been an imperative rule. Its wisdom and necessity received a triumphant confirmation from the very outset of the riots ; for, in their steady discipline, prompt military movements and obedience to command, was the strength and safety of the force. Acting together, moving as one man, they, numerically weak, overcame odds counting by thousands. This discipline is mainly due to General JAMES BOWEN, who, as one of the Commissioners, early saw its necessity and devoted himself to its enforcement. Gen. BOWEN was in New Orleans during the riots, but has had the gratification of hearing that what he initiated has been valuably perfected.

The conduct of the force exceeded the expectations of Commissioners ACTON and BERGEN. They did expect much from them, but their readiness and willingness on all occasions and at all hours, their uncomplaining response to every call, their cheerful endurance of fatigue, and a gallantry which knew no hesitancy, are subjects of their enthusiastic pride and encomiums.

In testimony of the invaluable services of the police have been scores of complimentary letters from prominent sources. As one of the handsomest acknowledgments, because from one who had full opportunity of judging, is the following from Brig.-Gen. HARVEY BROWN. He was in command of the military from Tuesday until Saturday of Riot

Week. It is a manly, frank, and generous acknowledgment from a gallant and accomplished officer. The extract is from a letter in response to one from a large number of prominent citizens complimentary to the judgment and energy displayed and the great services rendered by the General during the crisis:

FORT HAMILTON, August 6, 1863.

To Shepherd Knapp, George Opdyke, Leonard W. Jerome, Moses Taylor, Esqs., and others:

GENTLEMEN : I beg you to accept my grateful thanks for the kind and flattering letter with which you have honored me.

The only merit I can claim, in the performance of the duty which has given me the high distinction of your approbation, is that of an honest singleness of purpose in seconding the very able and energetic efforts of the President of the Metropolitan Police, Mr. ACTON, to whom, in my opinion, more than to any other one man is due the credit of the early suppression of the riot.

I never for a moment forgot that to the police was confided the conservation of the peace of the City; and that only in conjunction with the city authorities, and on their requisition, could the United States forces be lawfully and properly employed in suppressing the riot, and in restoring that peace and good order which had been so lawlessly broken. Acting in accordance with this principle, and as aids to the gallant City Police, the officers and soldiers of my command performed the most unpleasant and arduous duty, with that prompt energy and fearless patriotism which may ever be expected from the soldiers of the Republic.

On the week after the riot the Board of Police Commissioners issued the following Address to the force, in which a well-earned tribute is paid to the Military.

To the Metropolitan Police Force.

On the morning of Monday, the 13th inst., the peace and good order of the city was broken by a mob collected in several quarters of the city, for the avowed purpose of resisting the process of drafting names to recruit the armies of the Union.

Vast crowds of men collected and fired the offices where drafting was in progress, beating and driving the officers from duty.

From the beginning, these violent proceedings were accompanied by arson, robbery, and murder.

Private property, unofficial persons of all ages, sexes, and conditions, were indiscriminately assailed—none were spared, except those who were supposed by the mob to sympathize with their proceedings.

Early in the day the Superintendent was assaulted, cruelly beaten, robbed and disabled by the mob which was engaged in burning the Provost Marshal's office in Third Avenue, thus in a manner disarranging the organization at the Central Department, throwing new, unwonted, and responsible duties upon the Board.

At this juncture the telegraph wires of the department were cut, and the movement of forces by the railroads and stages violently interrupted, interfering seriously with our accustomed means of transmitting orders and concentrating forces.

The militia of the city were absent at the seat of war, fighting the battles of the nation against treason and secession, and there was no adequate force in the city for the first twelve hours to resist at all points the vast and infuriated mob. The police force was not strong enough in any precinct to make head, unaided, against the overwhelming force. No course was left but to concentrate the whole force at the Central Department, and thence send detachments able to encounter and conquer the rioters. This course was promptly adopted on Monday morning. The military were called upon to act in aid of the civil force to subdue the treasonable mob, protect life and property, and restore public order.

Under such adverse circumstances you were called upon to encounter a mob of such strength as have never before been seen in this country. The force of militia under General SANDFORD, who were called into service by the authority of this Board, were concentrated by him at and held the Arsenal in Seventh Avenue, throughout the contest. The military forces in command of Brevet Brigadier-General HARVEY BROWN reported at the Central Department, and there General BROWN established his head-quarters, and from there expeditions, combined of police and military force, were sent out that in all cases conquered, defeated or dispersed the mob force, and subjected them to severe chastisement. In no instance did these detachments from the Central Department, whether of police alone, or police and military combined, meet with defeat or serious check.

In all cases they achieved prompt and decisive victories. The contest continued through Monday, Tuesday, Wednesday, Thursday, and till 11 o'clock on Thursday night, like a continuous battle, when it ended by a total and sanguinary route of the insurgents.

During the whole of those anxious days and nights, Brig.-Gen. BROWN remained at the Central Department, ordering the movements of the military in carefully considered combinations with the police force, and throughout the struggle, and until its close, commanded the admiration and gratitude of the Police Department and all who witnessed his firm intelligence and soldierly conduct.

It is understood that he had at no time under his immediate command more than three hundred troops, but they were of the highest order, and were commanded by officers of courage and ability. They cordially acted with, supported, and were supported by the police, and victory in every contest against fearful odds was the result of brave fighting and intelligent command.

In the judgment of this Board, the escape of the city from the power of an infuriated mob is due to the aid furnished the police by Brig.-Gen. BROWN and the small military force under his command. No one can doubt, who saw him as we did, that during those anxious and eventful days and nights Brig.-Gen. HARVEY BROWN was equal to the situation, and was the right man in the right place.

We avail ourselves of this occasion to tender to him in the most earnest and public manner the thanks of the department and our own.

To the soldiers under his command we are grateful as to brave men who periled all to save the city from a reign of terror. To Captains PUT-

NAM, FRANKLIN and SHELLY, Lieut. RYER and Lieut.-Col. BERENS, officers of corps under the command of Brig.-Gen. BROWN, we are especially indebted, and we only discharge a duty when we commend them to their superiors in rank and to the War Department for their courageous and effective service.

Of the Inspectors, Captains, and Sergeants of police who led parties in the fearful contest, we are proud to say that none faltered or failed. Each was equal to the hour and the emergency. Not one failed to overcome the danger, however imminent, or to defeat the enemy, however numerous. Especial commendation is due to Drill-Sergeant COPELAND for his most valuable aid in commanding the movements of larger detachments of the police.

The patrolmen who were on duty fought through the numerous and fierce conflicts with the steady courage of veteran soldiers, and have won, as they deserve, the highest commendations from the public and from this Board. In their ranks there was neither faltering nor straggling. Devotion to duty and courage in the performance of it were universal.

The public and the department owe a debt of gratitude to the citizens who voluntarily became special patrolmen, some three thousand of whom, for several days and nights, did regular patrolman's duty with great effect. In the name of the public and of the department in which they were volunteers we thank them.

Mr. Crowley, the Superintendent of the police telegraph, and the attaches of his department, by untiring and sleepless vigilance in transmitting information by telegraph unceasingly through more than ten days and nights, have more than sustained the high reputation they have always possessed.

Through all these bloody contests, through all the wearing fatigue and wasting labor, you have demeaned yourselves like worthy members of the Metropolitan Police.

The public judgment will commend and reward you. A kind Providence has permitted you to escape with less casualties than could have been expected. You have lost one comrade, whom you have buried with honor. Your wounded will, it is hoped, all recover, to join you and share your honors. It is hoped that the severe, but just, chastisement which has been inflicted upon those guilty of riot, pillage, arson and murder, will deter further attempts of that character. But if, arising out of political or other causes, there should be another attempt to interrupt public order, we shall call on you again to crush its authors, confident that you will respond like brave men, as you ever have, to the calls of duty; and in future, whenever the attempt may be made, you will have to aid you large forces of military, ably commanded, and thus be enabled to crush in the bud any attempted riot or revolution.

To General CANBY, who, on the morning of Friday, the 17th inst., took command of the military, relieving Brig.-Gen. BROWN, and to Gen. DIX, who succeeded Gen. WOOL, the public are indebted for prompt, vigorous and willing aid to the police force in all the expeditions which have been called for since they assumed their commands. Charged particularly with the protection of the immense amount of Federal property and interests in the Metropolitan district, and the police force charged with the maintenance of public order, the duties of the two forces are always coincident.

Whatever menaces or disturbs one equally menaces and disturbs the other.

We are happy to know that at all times the several authorities have co-operated with that concert and harmony which is necessary to secure vigor and efficiency in action.

Sergeant YOUNG of the detective force, aided by Mr. NEWCOMB and other special patrolmen, rendered most effective service in arranging the commissary supplies for the large number of police, military, special patrolmen, and destitute colored refugees, whose subsistence was thrown unexpectedly on the department. The duty was arduous and responsible, and was performed with vigor and fidelity. All the clerks of the department, each in his sphere, performed a manly share of the heavy duties growing out of these extraordinary circumstances. The Central Department became a home of refuge for large numbers of poor, persecuted colored men, women, and children, many of whom were wounded and sick, and all of whom were helpless, exposed, and poor. Mr. JOHN H. KEYSER, with his accustomed philanthropy, volunteered, and was appointed to superintend these wretched victims of violence and prejudice, and has devoted unwearied days to the duty. The pitiable condition of these poor people appeals in the strongest terms to the Christian charity of the benevolent and humane. The members of the force will do an acceptable service by calling the attention to their condition of those who are able and willing to contribute in charity to their relief.

On the 10th of August, the Inspectors, after receipt of the reports from the different Captains, submitted the following to the Police Commissioners, with which the "Record" will close.

OFFICE OF INSPECTORS, }
NEW YORK, August 10th, 1863. }

JOHN A. KENNEDY, ESQ., *Superintendent:*

SIR,—The undersigned respectfully beg leave to submit the reports of the several Captains of the Metropolitan Police who were in command of precincts within the City of New York during the memorable Week of Riot, viz.: from July 13th to July 18th, both inclusive. Also, reports of several Sergeants, comprising a detailed account of the duty performed by their respective commands during the same week; one by Sergeant BRACKETT of the Twenty-first Precinct, who, by the order of President ACTON, had command of that precinct from the morning of the 16th of July, Captain PALMER having reported sick on the afternoon of the preceding day; others who had separate commands requiring a separate report.

The reports of the Captains and Sergeants are so elaborate and full in detail that the undersigned do not deem it necessary to make separate reports.

Each report is a truthful record of the arduous duties most cheerfully and heroically performed by their commands, and in the aggregate will form a most creditable and honorable epoch in the history of the Metropolitan Police.

The undersigned take this occasion to tender their sincere thanks to the Captains, Sergeants, and Patrolmen of the Metropolitan Police for the faithful manner in which they performed the most trying duty that was ever performed by any police force in this country, and was probably never excelled by the police force of any city in the world. We cannot, in a report of this kind point out single instances of bravery, coolness and endurance, where it was shown so universally : And besides, while single instances came under our immediate observation which would be in consonance with our feelings to refer to them, yet we fear would be doing injustice to others equally entitled to receive the same meed of praise. We were placed in a position where the whole field had to be looked over, hence we refer you to the reports alluded to, and where in many instances special mention is made of meritorious conduct.

Two of the undersigned, however (viz.: Inspectors CARPENTER and DILKS—Inspector LEONARD, having command of the force at the City Hall, did not have the opportunity of witnessing what we did) cannot in justice pass unnoticed the faithful and valuable services of Drill-Instructor Sergeant T. S. COPELAND. He was with us at the Central Office from the commencement to the termination of the riot, and greatly facilitated us in forming battalions to send to meet the mob. He accompanied one of the undersigned (Inspector CARPENTER) in all the attacks he made upon the rioters, and in which he displayed great coolness and courage, being always in advance, and demonstrated the excellent state of discipline he had drilled the force up to.

In closing, the undersigned wish to state that in all cases where they were ordered to proceed with large bodies of the force to meet and repel the mob, whether accompanied with military or not, the officers and men performed their whole duty, far exceeding our most sanguine expectations.

The undersigned cannot close this brief report without calling your particular attention to this significant fact, that out of a body of a little over two thousand men that comprise this force but few, very few, in any manner shrank from their trying duties. This, we think, will stand out as a most honorable mark of distinction for the members of the Metropolitan Police.

DANIEL CARPENTER, ⎫
GEO. W. DILKS,   ⎬ *Inspectors.*
JAS. LEONARD.   ⎭

NOTE.—The Captains of the several precincts made full and interesting reports to the Commissioners of the duties performed, during Riot Week, by their several commands. These reports have been referred to for the purposes of this compilation, and have been of great value in perfecting it.

THE COURT, JURIES, AND PROSECUTING OFFICERS.

Reference to the course of Recorder HOFFMAN, the Grand and Petit Juries, and the Prosecuting officers, on the indictment and trial of rioters, at the August Term of the Court of General Sessions—the only Court in session to the date of this publication at which the Riot cases could be tried—forms an appropriate sequel to the "Record."

The Court met on Monday, August 3d, and on the following day Recorder HOFFMAN delivered his charge. It was eloquent and earnest; he used no modifying language in speaking of the crimes which had been committed; no shady words in characterizing the criminals. Those who burn asylums, dwellings, stores, are guilty of arson; those who plunder are thieves; a rioter is an enemy of society, and the punishment due a murderer is death. To each and all of these classes the penalty which the law affixes, would, he said, be sternly meted out. In calling the attention of the Grand Jury to the riots, and urging them to a thorough, fearless examination of all cases of participation brought before them, the Recorder used the following language:

"We stand here, to-day, not as individuals, but as public officers charged with grave responsibilities. Let us not shrink from them. Let us remember that we are not partisans, but sworn officers of the law, determined at all hazards to enforce law and preserve order, to protect the innocent and punish the guilty."

The Grand Jury entered upon their laborious duties with the same spirit which characterized the charge, and performed them fearlessly and faithfully.

The District Attorney and his associates, SAMUEL B. GARVIN, in Court, and. ORLANDO L. STEWART, conducted the prosecutions, and urged them to success with unwearying energy and zeal. Of the twenty persons tried on charge of being concerned in the riots, nineteen were convicted.

The Petit Juries participated in the determination pervading the officials of the Court to thoroughly discharge their duty, and, by their unhesitating action and just findings, relieved the Jury Box of the imputations so often made against it.

Recorder HOFFMAN was stern and inflexible in his sentences. The aggregate time of imprisonment for the rioters sentenced at this term, which continued but ten days, was nearly one hundred years.

The action of this Court has satisfied the lawless that for them there is no more license, and has done more to encourage the police, to strengthen them in the discharge of their duty, than even the approval and laudations which have been showered upon them. It has also renewed the confidence of the community, and assured them that for crime there is punishment, and for criminals its certainty.

APPENDIX.

The following are some of the most atrocious cases of murder perpetrated by the rioters. The facts relating to some of the colored victims are condensed from the interesting Report of the Secretary of the Merchant's Relief Committee:

MURDER OF COL. O'BRIEN.

The murder of Col. H. J. O'BRIEN, by the mob, on the afternoon of Tuesday of Riot Week, was characterized by appalling barbarities. After the battle between the police under Inspector CARPENTER, in the Second Avenue, and after the police had left, Col. O'BRIEN, in command of two companies, 11th Regiment, N. Y. Vols., arrived at Thirty-fourth Street and Second Avenue. The rioters had reassembled, a collision ensued, and the military opened fire. The mob dispersed, and Col. O'BRIEN, leaving his command, walked up the avenue a short distance, entering a drug store. Returning to the street in a few moments, he was instantly surrounded by a vengeful and relentless crowd, which had re-collected, at once knocked down, beaten and mutilated shockingly till insensible. He thus lay for upwards of an hour, breathing heavily, and on any movement receiving kicks and stones. He was then taken by the heels, dragged around the street, and again left lying in it. For some four hours did he thus lay, subjected to infamous outrages, among them the occasional thrusting of a stick down his throat when gasping for breath. No one who did not seek to feed his brutality upon him was allowed to approach him. One man who sought to give him a drop of water was instantly set upon and barely escaped with his life. While still breathing, he was taken into the yard of his own house, near the scene, and there the most revolting atrocities were perpetrated, underneath which the life, that had so tenaciously clung to him, fled. No one could have recognized his remains. The murderers, satiated with their excess of fiendishness, left, and the body was allowed to be removed to Bellevue Hospital.

COLORED VICTIMS OF THE RIOT.

WM. HENRY NICHOLS (colored). Nichols resided at No. 147 East Twenty-eighth St. Mrs. STAAT, his mother, was visiting him. On Wednesday, July 15th, at 3 o'clock, the house was attacked by a mob with showers of bricks and stones. In one of the rooms was a woman with a child but

8

three days old. The rioters broke open the door with axes and rushed in. NICHOLS and his mother fled to the basement; in a few moments the babe referred to was dashed by the rioters from the upper window into the yard, and instantly killed. The mob cut the water pipes above, and the basement was being deluged; ten persons, mostly women and children, were there, and they fled to the yard; in attempting to climb the fence Mrs. STAATS fell back from exhaustion; the rioters were instantly upon her; her son sprang to her rescue, exclaiming, "Save my mother, if you kill me." Two ruffians instantly seized him, each taking hold of an arm, while a third, armed with a crow-bar, calling upon them to hold his arms apart, deliberately struck him a savage blow on the head, felling him like a bullock. He died in the N. Y. Hospital two days after.

JAMES COSTELLO (col'd).—JAMES COSTELLO, No. 97 West Thirty-third Street, killed on Tuesday morning, July 14th. COSTELLO was a shoemaker, an active man in his business, industrious and sober. He went out early in the morning upon an errand, was accosted, and finally was pursued by a powerful man. He ran down the street; endeavored to make his escape; was nearly overtaken by his pursuer; in self-defence he turned and shot the rioter with a revolver. The shot proved to be mortal; he died two days after. COSTELLO was immediately set upon by the mob. They first mangled his body, then hanged it. They then cut down his body and dragged it through the gutters, smashing it with stones, and finally burnt it. The mob then attempted to kill Mrs. COSTELLO and her children, but she escaped by climbing fences and taking refuge in a police station-house.

ABRAHAM FRANKLIN (colored).—This young man, who was murdered by the mob on the corner of Twenty-seventh Street and Seventh Avenue, was a quiet, inoffensive man, of unexceptionable character. He was a cripple, but supported himself and his mother, being employed as a coachman. A short time previous to the assault, he called upon his mother to see if anything could be done by him for her safety. The old lady said she considered herself perfectly safe; but if her time to die had come, she was ready to die. Her son then knelt down by her side, and implored the protection of Heaven in behalf of his mother. The old lady said that it seemed to her that good angels were present in the room. Scarcely had the supplicant risen from his knees, when the mob broke down the door, seized him, beat him over the head and face with fists and clubs, and then hanged him in the presence of his parent. While they were thus engaged the military came and drove them away, cutting down the body of FRANKLIN, who raised his arm once slightly and gave a few signs of life. The military then moved on to quell other riots, when the mob returned and again suspended the now probably lifeless body of FRANKLIN, cutting out pieces of flesh, and otherwise shockingly mutilating it.

AUGUSTUS STUART (colored).—Died at Hospital, Blackwell's Island, July 22, from the effects of a blow received at the hands of the mob, on Wednesday evening of Riot Week. He had been badly beaten previously by a band of rioters, and was frightened and insane from the effects of the blows which he had received. He was running toward the Arsenal

(State), Seventh Avenue and Thirty-seventh Street, for safety, when he was overtaken by the mob, from whom he received his death blow.

PETER HEUSTON.—PETER HEUSTON, sixty-three years of age, a Mohawk Indian, dark complexion, but straight hair, and for several years a resident of New York, proved a victim to the riots. HEUSTON served with the New York Volunteers in the Mexican war. He was brutally attacked and shockingly beaten, on the 13th of July, by a gang of ruffians, who thought him to be of the African race because of his dark complexion. He died within four days, at Bellevue Hospital, from his injuries.

→ JEREMIAH ROBINSON (colored).—He was killed in Madison near Catharine Street. His widow stated that her husband, in order to escape, dressed himself in some of her clothes, and, in company with herself and one other woman, left their residence and went toward one of the Brooklyn ferries. ROBINSON wore a hood, which failed to hide his beard. Some boys, seeing his beard, lifted up the skirts of his dress, which exposed his heavy boots. Immediately the mob set upon him, and the atrocities they perpetrated are so revolting that they are unfit for publication. They finally killed him, and threw his body into the river. His wife and her companion ran up Madison street, and escaped across the Grand Street Ferry to Brooklyn.

WILLIAM JONES (colored).—A crowd of rioters in Clarkson Street, in pursuit of a negro, who in self-defence had fired on some rowdies, met an inoffensive colored man returning from a bakery with a loaf of bread under his arm. They instantly set upon and beat him and, after nearly killing him, hung him to a lamp-post. His body was left suspended for several hours. A fire was made underneath him, and he was literally roasted as he hung, the mob reveling in their demoniac act. Recognition of the remains, on their being recovered, was impossible; and two women mourned for upwards of two weeks, in the case of this man, for the loss of their husbands. At the end of that time, the husband of one of the mourners, to her great joy, returned like one recovered from the grave. The principal evidence which the widow, Mary Jones, had to identify the murdered man as her husband, was the fact of his having a loaf of bread under his arm, he having left the house to get a loaf of bread a few minutes before the attack.

JOSEPH REED (colored).—This was a lad of seven years of age, residing at No. 147 East Twenty-eighth Street, with an aged grandmother and widowed mother. On Wednesday morning of the fearful week, a crowd of ruffians gathered in the neighborhood, determined on a work of plunder and death. They attacked the house, stole everything they could carry with them, and, after threatening the inmates, set fire to it. The colored people, who had the sole occupancy of the building, fled in confusion into the midst of the gathering crowd. And then the child was separated from his guardians. His youth and evident illness, even from the devils around him, it would be thought, should have insured his safety. But no sooner did they see his unprotected, defenceless condition, than a gang of fiendish men seized him, beat him with sticks, and bruised him with heavy cobble-stones. But one, ten-fold more the servant of Satan than the rest, rushed at the child, and with the stock of a pistol struck him on the temple and felled him to the ground. A noble young fireman, by the name of JOHN F. GOVERN, of No. 39 Hose Company, instantly came to the rescue, and, single-handed, held the crowd at bay. Taking the wounded and unconscious boy in his arms, he carried him to a place of safety. The terrible beating and the great fright the poor lad had undergone was too much for his feeble frame; he died on the following Tuesday.

JOSEPH JACKSON (colored), aged 19 years, living in West Fifty-third Street, near Sixth Avenue, was in the industrious pursuit of his humble occupation of gathering provender for a herd of cattle, and when near the foot of Thirty-fourth Street, East River, July 15, was set upon by the mob, killed, and his body thrown into the river.

SAMUEL JOHNSON (colored).—On Tuesday night JOHNSON was attacked near Fulton Ferry by a gang who mercilessly beat and left him for dead. A proposition was made to throw him into the river, but for some reason the murderers took fright and fled. He was taken by some citizens to his home, and died the next day.

—— WILLIAMS (colored).—He was attacked on the corner of Le Roy and Washington Streets, on Tuesday morning, July 14th, knocked down, a number of men jumped upon, kicked, and stamped upon him until insensible. One of the murderers knelt on the body and drove a knife into it; the blade being too small he threw it away and resorted to his fists. Another seized a huge stone, weighing near twenty pounds, and deliberately crushed it again and again on to the victim. A force of police, under Captain DICKSON, arrived and rescued the man, who was conveyed to the New York Hospital. He was only able to articulate " WILLIAMS " in response to a question as to his name, and remained insensible thereafter, dying in a few days.

ANN DERRICKSON.—This was a white woman, the wife of a colored man, and lived at No. 11 York Street. On Wednesday, July 15th, the rioters seized a son of deceased, a lad of about twelve years, saturated his clothes and hair with camphene, and then procuring a rope, fastened one end to a lamp-post, the other around his neck, and were about to set him on fire, and hang him; they were interfered with by some citizens and by the police of the First Ward, and their diabolical attempt at murder frustrated. While Mrs. DERRICKSON was attempting to save the life of her son she was horribly bruised and beaten with a cart rung. The victim, after lingering three or four weeks, died from the effects of her injuries.

BURNING OF THE COLORED ORPHAN ASYLUM.

About 4 o'clock on the afternoon of Monday, July 13th, a mob of some three thousand attacked the Asylum for Colored Orphans on Fifth Avenue. The main building was four stories, with wings of three stories, and was capable of accommodating five hundred children. With the grounds, it extended from Forty-third to Forty-fourth Street. At the time the mob came upon it, there were, besides the officers and matrons, over two hundred children in it, from infancy to twelve years of age. Superintendent WM. E. DAVIS hurriedly fastened the doors, and while the mob were breaking them in the children were collected, and then escaped by the rear just as the ruffians had effected their entrance in front. Those entering at once proceeded to ransack and pillage every room in the building. Everything that could be was stolen, even to the dresses and trinkets of the orphans. What could not be carried off was destroyed. Meantime Chief Engineer DECKER reached the scene, and forced his way to the building. In attempting to address the mob, he was twice knocked down and finally forced into Fifth Avenue. Here some ten firemen joined him, and it was resolved to save the Asylum if possible. They boldly forced their way to and into the building. Here they were joined by Assistant Engineers LAMB and LEWIS. The chairs, desks, &c., had been broken up, piled in different parts of the building, and fires had been kindled on the first and second floors. The firemen scattered and extinguished all of them, and intimidated the rioters. Meanwhile some of the latter had succeeded in effectually firing the loft in every part; the demonstration against the chief and his small band of associates had become too formidable; to save the building was impossible, and they reluctantly yielded it to the mob, who, with exulting yells, soon saw the Asylum wrapped in flames. In an hour and a half only a small portion of the walls remained.

The firemen who acted so gallantly with the Chief and his Assistants were members of Hook and Ladder Company No. 2, Hose Company No. 31, Engine Companies Nos. 7, 9, and 10.

After their escape from the building, the Orphans were hurried in mournful procession to the Twentieth Precinct, Captain WALLING, where they were sheltered and provided for until their removal to Blackwell's Island. Except the clothes they wore, not an article was saved for them. The loss to the Society in building, furniture, and clothing was estimated at $80,000.

INDEX.

	PAGE
Commissioners	7
Chief Clerk	9
Superintendent	9
Inspectors	12, 17, 20, 23
Telegraph Bureau	25
Detective Force	29
First Precinct	32
Second Precinct	34
Third Precinct	36
Fourth Precinct	38
Fifth Precinct	40
Sixth Precinct	42
Seventh Precinct	44
Eighth Precinct	46
Ninth Precinct	48
Tenth Precinct	49
Eleventh Precinct	50
Twelfth Precinct	52
Thirteenth Precinct	54
Fourteenth Precinct	55
Fifteenth Precinct	57
Sixteenth Precinct	61
Seventeenth Precinct	63
Eighteenth Precinct	64
Nineteenth Precinct	67
Twentieth Precinct	68
Twenty-first Precinct	71
Twenty-second Precinct	73
Twenty-third Precinct	74
Twenty-fourth Precinct	76
Twenty-fifth Precinct	78
Twenty-sixth Precinct	81
Twenty-seventh Precinct	86
Twenty-eighth Precinct	90
Twenty-ninth Precinct	93
Thirtieth Precinct	96
Thirty-first Precinct	97
Thirty-second Precinct	98
Sanitary Police	100
Drill Officer	103
Superintendent and Inspectors' Offices	105
Brooklyn Precincts	105
Brig.-Gen. Harvey Brown	107
Commissioners' Address to Force, and acknowledgment to the Military	107
Inspectors' Report	110
Court, Juries, and Prosecuting Officers	112
The Murders	113
Burning of the Colored Orphan Asylum	117

www.ingramcontent.com/pod-product-compliance
Lightning Source LLC
Chambersburg PA
CBHW030626270326
41927CB00007B/1328